Presented to

On

By

Martin Luther's Small and Large Catechisms

CONCORDIA PUBLISHING HOUSE · SAINT LOUIS

Copyright © 2019 Concordia Publishing House
3558 S. Jefferson Ave., St. Louis, MO 63118-3968
1-800-325-3040 · cph.org

Manufactured in the United States of America

1 2 3 4 5 6 7 8 9 10   34 33 32 31 30 29 28 27 26 25

CONTENTS

EDITOR'S INTRODUCTION TO THE CATECHISMS

> God Himself is not ashamed to teach these things daily. He knows nothing better to teach. . . . Can we finish learning in one hour what God Himself cannot finish teaching?
>
> —Martin Luther (LC Preface 16)

Echoing the Truth: What Does *Catechesis* Mean?

The term *catechism* comes from the Greek word *katecho*, which literally means to "sound back and forth." (The word *echo* also comes from this Greek word.) Thus the "catechetical" method of teaching is rooted in classical Greek and Roman educational methods and was used throughout the Middle Ages down to Luther's time: The teacher asks a question; the student responds with a fixed and set answer, and so it goes, echoing back and forth. Repetition and recitation of the material is used to instill in the student the words, phrases, and concepts being taught. An explanation is also added, according to the student's level of understanding. In this way, the Christian Church taught, or *catechized*, the faith. The students learning the faith are known as *catechumens,* and they receive careful and thorough *catechesis* (instruction) in the Christian faith.

The Catechism in the Middle Ages

In Luther's day there were any number of catechisms and catechetical materials. They were often extremely extensive and required the young people to memorize not only the Ten Commandments, the Lord's Prayer, and the Creed, but also a list of seven spiritual gifts, seven cardinal virtues, the seven Sacraments, seven words of mercy, the eight beatitudes of God, and on and on and on. Luther cleared away the medieval clutter and retained the core texts of the catechisms: The Ten Commandments, the Creed, and the Lord's Prayer. He then added explanations to Baptism, Absolution, and the Sacrament of the Altar. Instead of prayers to Mary and the saints, Luther provided prayers for the beginning and end of the day, and also prayers before and after meals. Luther's goal with his Small Catechism was to provide something that was much shorter, easier to teach and to learn, memorable, and to the point. The Large Catechism was designed by Luther to provide more information and further material both for teachers and learners. Luther's hope was that students who had mastered the Small Catechism would move on to the Large Catechism.

The Origin of the Catechisms

Martin Luther was first and foremost a Bible professor at the University of Wittenberg, but he was also a parish preacher who served at both the city and castle churches in Wittenberg. In 1516 Luther preached a thorough sermon series on the Ten Commandments. In 1517 he preached a sermon series on the Lord's Prayer and wrote a short explanation of the Ten Commandments to help the members of the parish confess their sins. In 1518 Luther published his exposition of the Ten Commandments. In the next two years he published other short tracts based on his catechetical sermons. In 1520 he gathered these resources together and had them published under the title *A Short Form of the Ten Commandments, the Creed, and the Lord's Prayer.*

Luther wanted this book to serve the laypeople. While Luther built on catechetical customs, his work stood out as a clear departure from much of medieval catechesis. There were three key reasons for this: First, Luther removed a lot of the additional materials that had accumulated throughout the Middle Ages and focused primarily on the Ten Commandments, the Creed, and the Lord's Prayer, urging that if these three things were learned well, the most important truths of Christianity would be known. Second, Luther very intentionally arranged the catechism so that the Commandments would be first, then the Creed, then the Lord's Prayer. Third, Luther divided the Apostles' Creed into only three parts, not the traditional twelve parts. Luther wanted to focus clearly on the three persons of the Holy Trinity and their respective saving work. Luther's little 1520 book was the foundation for his later catechetical work.

In 1525 Luther formally commissioned what he called the "children's catechism" (*catechismus pueroum)*, using the term *catechism* for the first time. He directed his colleagues Justus Jonas and John Agricola to do this work. Luther felt he was too busy to do it himself, but as it turned out, Jonas and Agricola also did not do the job to Luther's satisfaction.

Luther continued preaching each year on the basic parts of the catechism and added sermons equally clear and simple on the Sacraments:

Baptism, Absolution, and the Lord's Supper. In 1528 he again took over catechism instruction in the parish church in Wittenberg and preached three series of sermons that year—in May, September, and December—each containing about ten sermons. These thirty sermons would serve Luther well a year later, in 1529, when he finally wrote the catechisms.

What ignited Luther's passion to put the catechisms in writing was a visit he had made to Saxony at the urging of its Elector. Luther was horrified to see how bad things were in the Saxon churches. He realized how essential it was for him to get to work on his catechisms. Here is what he said:

> The deplorable, miserable condition which I discovered lately when I, too, was a visitor, has forced and urged me to prepare this Catechism, or Christian doctrine, in this small, plain, simple form. Mercy! Good God! what manifold misery I beheld! The common people . . . have no knowledge whatever of Christian doctrine, and, alas! many pastors are altogether incapable, and incompetent to teach. Nevertheless, all maintain that they are Christians. . . . Yet they cannot recite either the Lord's Prayer, or the Creed, or the Ten Commandments, they live like dumb brutes and irrational swine. (Bente, 156)

Luther finished the Large Catechism in March 1529, and in mid-April the first copies were in print. The title was simply *German Catechism, Martin Luther.* He finished the Small Catechism in May 1529. Its title was *The Small Catechism for Ordinary Pastors and Preachers. Martin Luther. Wittenberg.* It was an instant best-seller, printed and reprinted many times in Wittenberg and other cities throughout Germany. In early 1529 Luther also had large posters printed containing the chief parts of the catechism. These posters were hung up on walls in churches, schools, and homes for the people to recite together.

Marriage and Baptismal Booklets

After the first printing of the catechisms, Luther added a few things, such as a short form for Confession, and orders for baptismal and wedding services. The main portions of the Small Catechism, first produced in 1529, were never essentially changed.

When the Book of Concord was prepared in 1580, there were disagreements about what to include with the Small Catechism. The Marriage and Baptismal Booklets had, early on, been included in editions of the Small Catechism and were particularly well liked by the Saxons and others in Northern Germany. Therefore, in the first drafts of the Book of Concord, the Marriage Booklet and the Baptismal Booklet were included as part of Luther's Small Catechism. However, Jacob Andreae explained that their inclusion was the result of an editorial mistake, perhaps by a proofreader at the printer. Andreae removed them, leaving only a bit of the liturgical service (but not the doctrinal portions of those documents). Because Andreae left a portion of the Marriage and Baptismal Booklets in the book, Duke Julius of Braunschweig-Wolfenbüttel noticed and expressed his concern. Prince John George of Brandenburg also wanted them included, insisting that the Small Catechism be printed in the Book of Concord "without truncation." While the Saxons and others in Northern Germany wanted both of these little booklets included in the Small Catechism, Lutherans in Southern Germany did not. They regarded them as nonessential to the unity of the Church and expressed concerns about the exorcism in the baptismal rite. Additional concerns were expressed about mandating a precise liturgical order for Baptism and marriage and also for making a precise liturgical order mandatory and part of the Lutheran Church's formal Confessions.

Martin Chemnitz was able to resolve the disagreements by suggesting that the official copies of the Book of Concord deposited in the princely courts and libraries not contain the Marriage and Baptismal Booklets. Instead, the official copies would include blank pages where these could be inserted if a Lutheran territory wanted to have them as part of its church order. For example, two of the three official copies of the 1580 Book of Concord deposited in the state archives of Saxony, in Dresden, do not include the Marriage and Baptismal Booklets. Soon the Book of Concord was printed without the blank pages to mark where the Marriage and Baptismal Booklets would be in the Small Catechism. For these reasons, they were not included in *Concordia: The Lutheran Confessions* or this compilation of the catechisms, even as they were not included in the *Concordia Triglotta.*

The text of the Small Catechism in this work is the 1986 translation. The text of the Large Catechism is from the 1580 German edition of the Book of Concord, which was the base text for the catechisms in the *Concordia Triglotta.*

TIMELINE

1516	Luther preaches sermon series on Ten Commandments
1517	Luther preaches sermon series on Lord's Prayer; posts Ninety-five Theses
1521	Luther excommunicated by papal bull *Decet Romanum Pontificem*; appears before Diet of Worms; refuses to recant, stating, "Here I stand"
1524	Peasants' War begins, led in part by Thomas Münzer
1525	Luther asks Justus Jonas and John Agricola to produce a "catechism"
	Luther marries Katharina von Bora, June 13
1526	Diet of Speyer grants German princes right to establish religion in their territory
	Church visitation begins to assess needs of congregations
1527	Visitation articles prepared
	Plague strikes Wittenberg; Luther and Katharina turn their home into a hospital

1528 Luther teaches catechism instruction at the parish church; preaches three-sermon series on parts of catechism

1529 Luther publishes the *Large Catechism* in April and the *Small Catechism* in May

1530 *Augsburg Confession* presented to Charles V at Diet of Augsburg, June 25

OUTLINE OF SMALL CATECHISM

Preface

I. The Ten Commandments

II. The Creed

III. The Lord's Prayer

IV. The Sacrament of Holy Baptism

V. Confession

VI. The Sacrament of the Altar

Daily Prayers

Table of Duties

Enchiridion
The Small Catechism

PREFACE OF DR. MARTIN LUTHER

Martin Luther to all faithful and godly pastors and preachers: grace, mercy, and peace in Jesus Christ, our Lord.

1 The deplorable, miserable condition that I
discovered recently when I, too, was a visitor, has
forced and urged me to prepare this catechism,
or Christian doctrine, in this small, plain, simple
2 form. Mercy! Dear God, what great misery I
beheld! The common person, especially in the
villages, has no knowledge whatever of Christian
doctrine. And unfortunately, many pastors are
completely unable and unqualified to teach. ‹This
is so much so, that one is ashamed to speak of it.›
3 Yet, everyone says that they are Christians, have
been baptized, and receive the holy Sacraments,
even though they cannot even recite the Lord's
Prayer or the Creed or the Ten Commandments.
They live like dumb brutes and irrational hogs.
Now that the Gospel has come, they have nicely
learned to abuse all freedom like experts.

O bishops! What answer will you ever give to Christ for having so shamefully neglected the people and never for a moment fulfilled your office [James 3:1]? May all misfortune run from you! ‹I do not wish at this place to call down evil on your heads.› You command the Sacrament in one form and insist on your human laws, and yet at the same time you do not care at all whether the people know the Lord's Prayer, the Creed, the Ten Commandments, or any part of God's Word. Woe, woe to you forever! [See Matthew 23.] 4

Therefore, I beg you all for God's sake, my dear sirs and brethren, who are pastors or preachers, to devote yourselves heartily to your office [1 Timothy 4:13]. Have pity on the people who are entrusted to you [Acts 20:28] and help us teach the catechism to the people, and especially to the young. And let those of you who cannot do better take these tables and forms and impress them, word for word, on the people [Deuteronomy 6:7], as follows: 6

In the first place, let the preacher above all be careful to avoid many versions or various texts and forms of the Ten Commandments, the Lord's Prayer, the Creed, the Sacraments, and such. He should choose one form to which he holds and teaches all the time, year after year. For young 7 and simple people must be taught by uniform, settled texts and forms. Otherwise they become confused easily when the teacher today teaches them one way, and in a year some other way, as if he wished to make improvements. For then all effort and labor ‹that has been spent in teaching› is lost.

8 Our blessed fathers understood this well also. They all used the same form of the Lord's Prayer, the Creed, and the Ten Commandments. Therefore, we, too, should ‹be at pains to› teach the young and simple people these parts in such a way that we do not change a syllable or set them forth and repeat them one year differently than in another.

9 Therefore, choose whatever form you please, and hold to it forever. But when you preach in the presence of learned and intelligent people, you may show your skill. You may present these parts in varied and intricate ways and give them as masterly turns as you are able. But with the young people stick to one fixed, permanent form
10 and manner. Teach them, first of all, these parts: the Ten Commandments, the Creed, the Lord's Prayer, and so on, according to the text, word for word, so that they, too, can repeat it in the same way after you and commit it to memory.

But those who are unwilling to learn the cat- 11
echism should be told that they deny Christ and
are not Christians. They should not be admitted
to the Sacrament, accepted as sponsors at Baptism, or practice any part of Christian freedom.
They should simply be turned back to the pope
and his officials, indeed, to the devil himself
[1 Corinthians 5:5]. Furthermore, their parents 12
and employers should refuse them food and
drink, and notify them that the prince will drive
such rude people from the country.

Although we cannot and should not force 13
anyone to believe, we should insist and encourage
the people. That way they will know what is right
and wrong for those among whom they dwell and
wish to make their living. For whoever desires to
live in a town must know and observe the town
laws, because he wishes to enjoy the protection
offered by the laws whether he is a believer or at
heart and in private a rascal or rogue.

In the second place, after they have learned 14
the text well, teach them the meaning also, so
that they know what it means. Again, choose the
form of these tables or some other brief uniform
method, whichever you like, and hold to it. Do 15
not change a single syllable, as was just said about
the text. Take your time in doing this. For it is not 16

necessary for you to explain all the parts at once, but one after the other. After they understand the First Commandment well, then explain the Second, and so on. Otherwise they will be overwhelmed, so that they will not be able to remember anything well.

17 In the third place, after you have taught them this short catechism, then take up the Large Catechism and give them also a richer and fuller knowledge. Here enlarge upon every commandment, ‹article,› petition, and part with its various works, uses, benefits, dangers, and injuries, as you find these abundantly stated in many books
18 written about these matters. In particular, urge the commandment or part that most suffers the greatest neglect among your people. For example, the Seventh Commandment, about stealing, must be strongly urged among mechanics and merchants, and even farmers and servants. For among these people many kinds of dishonesty and stealing prevail. So, too, you must drive home the Fourth Commandment among the children and the common people, so that they may be quiet and faithful, obedient and peaceable. You must always offer many examples from the Scriptures to show how God has punished or blessed such persons [Deuteronomy 28].

In this matter you should especially urge 19
magistrates and parents to rule well and to send
their children to school. Show them why it is their
duty to do this and what a damnable sin they
are committing if they do not do it. For by such
neglect they overthrow and destroy both God's
kingdom and that of the world. They act as the
worst enemies both of God and of people. Make 20
it very plain to them what an awful harm they are
doing if they will not help to train children to be
pastors, preachers, clerks‹, and to fill other offices
that we cannot do without in this life›. God will
punish them terribly for this failure. There is great
need to preach this. In this matter parents and
rulers are now sinning in unspeakable ways. The
devil, too, hopes to accomplish something cruel
because of these things.

Last, since the tyranny of the pope has been 21
abolished, people are no longer willing to go to
the Sacrament, and thus they despise it. Here
again encouragement is necessary, yet with this
understanding: We are to force no one to believe
or to receive the Sacrament. Nor should we set 22
up any law, time, or place for it. Instead, preach
in such a way that by their own will, without our
law, they will urge themselves and, as it were,
compel us pastors to administer the Sacrament.

This is done by telling them, "When someone does not seek or desire the Sacrament at least four times a year, it is to be feared that he despises the Sacrament and is not a Christian, just as a person is not a Christian who does not believe or hear the Gospel." For Christ did not say, "Leave this out, or, despise this," but, "Do this, as often as you drink it" [1 Corinthians 11:25], and other such words. Truly, He wants it done, and not entirely neglected and despised. "Do this," He says.

23 Now, whoever does not highly value the Sacrament shows that he has no sin, no flesh, no devil, no world, no death, no danger, no hell. In other words, he does not believe any such things, although he is in them up over his head and his ears and is doubly the devil's own. On the other hand, he needs no grace, no life, no paradise, no heaven, no Christ, no God, nor anything good. For if he believed that he had so much evil around him, and needed so much that is good, he would not neglect the Sacrament, by which such evil is remedied and so much good is bestowed. Nor would it be necessary to force him to go to the Sacrament by any law. He would come running and racing of his own will, would force himself, and beg that you must give him the Sacrament.

Therefore, you must not make any law about 24
this, as the pope does. Only set forth clearly the
benefit and harm, the need and use, the danger
and the blessing, connected with this Sacrament.
Then the people will come on their own without
you forcing them. But if they do not come, let
them go their way and tell them that such people
belong to the devil who do not regard nor feel
their great need and God's gracious help. But if 25
you do not urge this, or make a law or make it
bitter, it is your fault if they despise the Sacrament. What else could they be than lazy if you
sleep and are silent? Therefore, look to it, pastors 26
and preachers. Our office has now become a different thing from what it was under the pope. It
has now become a serious and saving office. So it
now involves much more trouble and labor, danger and trials. In addition, it gains little reward 27
and thanks in the world. But Christ Himself will
be our reward if we labor faithfully [see Genesis
15:1]. To this end may the Father of all grace help
us, to whom be praise and thanks forever through
Christ, our Lord! Amen.

I. THE TEN COMMANDMENTS

AS THE HEAD OF THE
FAMILY SHOULD TEACH THEM IN
A SIMPLE WAY TO HIS HOUSEHOLD

GIVING OF THE COMMANDMENTS
(EXODUS 19)

The First Commandment

WORSHIP OF THE GOLDEN CALF
(EXODUS 32)

You shall have no other gods.

What does this mean?

Answer: We should fear, love, and trust in God above all things.

The Second Commandment

THE SON OF SHELOMITH IS STONED FOR BLASPHEMY (LEVITICUS 24)

You shall not misuse the name of the LORD your God.

What does this mean?

Answer: We should fear and love God so that we do not curse, swear, use satanic arts, lie, or deceive by His name, but call upon it in every trouble, pray, praise, and give thanks.

The Third Commandment

HEARING AND DESPISING PREACHING AND HIS WORD (NUMBERS 15)

Remember the Sabbath day by keeping it holy.

What does this mean?

Answer: We should fear and love God so that we do not despise preaching and His Word, but hold it sacred and gladly hear and learn it.

The Fourth Commandment

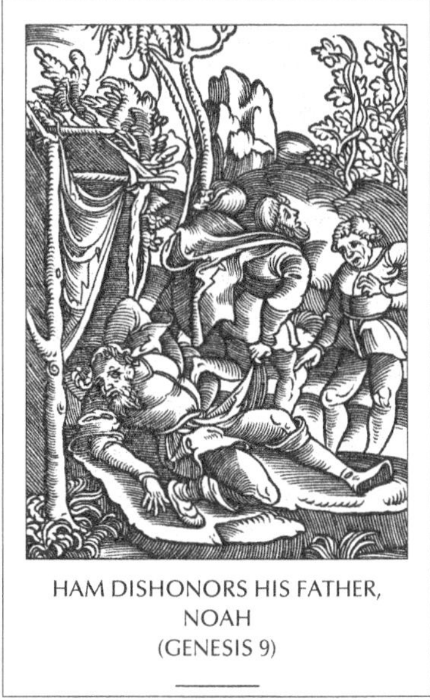

HAM DISHONORS HIS FATHER, NOAH
(GENESIS 9)

Honor your father and your mother.

What does this mean?

Answer: We should fear and love God so that we do not despise or anger our parents and other authorities, but honor them, serve and obey them, love and cherish them.

The Fifth Commandment

CAIN KILLS ABEL
(GENESIS 4)

You shall not murder.

What does this mean?

Answer: We should fear and love God so that we do not hurt or harm our neighbor in his body, but help and support him in every physical need.

The Sixth Commandment

DAVID AND BATHSHEBA
(2 SAMUEL 11)

You shall not commit adultery.

What does this mean?

Answer: We should fear and love God so that we lead a sexually pure and decent life in what we say and do, and husband and wife love and honor each other.

The Seventh Commandment

ACHAN THE THIEF
(JOSHUA 7)

You shall not steal.

What does this mean?

Answer: We should fear and love God so that we do not take our neighbor's money or possessions, or get them in any dishonest way, but help him to improve and protect his possessions and income.

The Eighth Commandment

BEARING FALSE WITNESS AGAINST SUSANNA (SUSANNA 34–41)

You shall not give false testimony against your neighbor.

What does this mean?

Answer: We should fear and love God so that we do not tell lies about our neighbor, betray him, slander him, or hurt his reputation, but defend him, speak well of him, and explain everything in the kindest way.

The Ninth Commandment

JACOB COVETS LABAN'S FLOCK
(GENESIS 30)

You shall not covet your neighbor's house.

What does this mean?

Answer: We should fear and love God so that we do not scheme to get our neighbor's inheritance or house, or get it in a way which only appears right, but help and be of service to him in keeping it.

The Tenth Commandment

JOSEPH FLEES POTIPHAR'S WIFE
(GENESIS 39)

You shall not covet your neighbor's wife, or his manservant or maidservant, his ox or donkey, or anything that belongs to your neighbor.

What does this mean?

Answer: We should fear and love God so that we do not entice or force away our neighbor's wife, workers, or animals, or turn them against him, but urge them to stay and do their duty.

[The text of the commandments is from Exodus 20:3, 7, 8, 12–17]

The Close of the Commandments

What does God say about all these commandments?

Answer:

He says, "I, the Lord your God, am a jealous God, punishing the children for the sin of the fathers to the third and fourth generation of those who hate Me, but showing love to a thousand generations of those who love Me and keep My commandments." (Exodus 20:5–6)

What does this mean?

Answer: God threatens to punish all who break these commandments. Therefore, we should fear His wrath and not do anything against them. But He promises grace and every blessing to all who keep these commandments. Therefore, we should also love and trust in Him and gladly do what He commands.

II. THE CREED

AS THE HEAD OF THE FAMILY SHOULD TEACH IT IN A SIMPLE WAY TO HIS HOUSEHOLD

THE HOLY TRINITY

The First Article

THE CREATION
(GENESIS 1)

Creation

I believe in God, the Father Almighty, Maker of heaven and earth.

What does this mean?

Answer: I believe that God has made me and all creatures; that He has given me my body and soul, eyes, ears, and all my members, my reason and all my senses, and still takes care of them.

He also gives me clothing and shoes, food and drink, house and home, wife and children, land, animals, and all I have. He richly and daily provides me with all that I need to support this body and life.

He defends me against all danger and guards and protects me from all evil.

All this He does only out of fatherly, divine goodness and mercy, without any merit or worthiness in me. For all this it is my duty to thank and praise, serve and obey Him.

This is most certainly true.

The Second Article

Redemption

And in Jesus Christ, His only Son, our Lord, who was conceived by the Holy Spirit, born of the Virgin Mary, suffered under Pontius Pilate, was crucified, died and was buried. He descended into hell. The third day He rose again from the dead. He ascended into heaven and sits at the right hand of God, the Father Almighty. From thence He will come to judge the living and the dead.

CHRIST CRUCIFIED (JOHN 19)

What does this mean?

Answer: I believe that Jesus Christ, true God, begotten of the Father from eternity, and also true man, born of the Virgin Mary, is my Lord,

who has redeemed me, a lost and condemned person, purchased and won me from all sins, from death, and from the power of the devil; not with gold or silver, but with His holy, precious blood and with His innocent suffering and death, that I may be His own and live under Him in His kingdom and serve Him in everlasting righteousness, innocence, and blessedness,

just as He is risen from the dead, lives and reigns to all eternity.

This is most certainly true.

The Third Article

PENTECOST (ACTS 2)

Sanctification

I believe in the Holy Spirit, the holy Christian church, the communion of saints, the forgiveness of sins, the resurrection of the body, and the life everlasting. Amen.

What does this mean?

Answer: I believe that I cannot by my own reason or strength believe in Jesus Christ, my Lord, or come to Him; but the Holy Spirit has called me by the Gospel, enlightened me with His gifts, sanctified and kept me in the true faith.

In the same way He calls, gathers, enlightens, and sanctifies the whole Christian church on earth, and keeps it with Jesus Christ in the one true faith.

In this Christian church He daily and richly forgives all my sins and the sins of all believers.

On the Last Day He will raise me and all the dead, and give eternal life to me and to all believers in Christ.

This is most certainly true.

III. THE LORD'S PRAYER

AS THE HEAD OF THE FAMILY SHOULD TEACH IT IN A SIMPLE WAY TO HIS HOUSEHOLD

The Introduction

Our Father who art in heaven.

Our Father in heaven.

JESUS TEACHES THE DISCIPLES TO PRAY (LUKE 11)

What does this mean?

Answer: With these words God tenderly invites us to believe that He is our true Father and that we are His true children, so that with all boldness and confidence we may ask Him as dear children ask their dear father.

The First Petition

Hallowed be Thy name.
Hallowed be Your name.

What does this mean?

Answer: God's name is certainly holy in itself, but we pray in this petition that it may be kept holy among us also.

CHRIST TEACHING (MATTHEW 5)

How is God's name kept holy?

Answer: God's name is kept holy when the Word of God is taught in its truth and purity, and we, as the children of God, also lead holy lives according to it. Help us to do this, dear Father in heaven! But anyone who teaches or lives contrary to God's Word profanes the name of God among us. Protect us from this, heavenly Father!

The Second Petition

Thy kingdom come.

Your kingdom come.

THE KINGDOM COMES
(LUKE 11)

What does this mean?

Answer: The kingdom of God certainly comes by itself without our prayer, but we pray in this petition that it may come to us also.

How does God's kingdom come?

Answer: God's kingdom comes when our heavenly Father gives us His Holy Spirit, so that by His grace we believe His holy Word and lead godly lives here in time and there in eternity.

The Third Petition

Thy will be done on earth as it is in heaven.

Your will be done on earth as in heaven.

What does this mean?

Answer: The good and gracious will of God is done even without our prayer, but we pray in this petition that it may be done among us also.

CHRIST DOING THE WILL OF THE FATHER (MATTHEW 27)

How is God's will done?

Answer: God's will is done

when He breaks and hinders every evil plan and purpose of the devil, the world, and our sinful nature, which do not want us to hallow God's name or let His kingdom come;

and when He strengthens and keeps us firm in His Word and faith until we die.

This is His good and gracious will.

The Fourth Petition

Give us this day our daily bread.

Give us today our daily bread.

FEEDING THE FIVE THOUSAND (JOHN 6)

What does this mean?

Answer: God certainly gives daily bread to everyone without our prayers, even to all evil people, but we pray in this petition that God would lead us to realize this and to receive our daily bread with thanksgiving.

What is meant by daily bread?

Answer: Daily bread includes everything that has to do with the support and needs of the body, such as food, drink, clothing, shoes, house, home, land, animals, money, goods, a devout husband or wife, devout children, devout workers, devout and faithful rulers, good government, good weather, peace, health, self-control, good reputation, good friends, faithful neighbors, and the like.

The Fifth Petition

And forgive us our trespasses as we forgive those who trespass against us.

Forgive us our sins as we forgive those who sin against us.

What does this mean?

THE UNMERCIFUL SERVANT (MATTHEW 18)

Answer: We pray in this petition that our Father in heaven would not look at our sins, or deny our prayer because of them. We are neither worthy of the things for which we pray, nor have we deserved them, but we ask that He would give them all to us by grace, for we daily sin much and surely deserve nothing but punishment. So we too will sincerely forgive and gladly do good to those who sin against us.

The Sixth Petition

And lead us not into temptation.

Lead us not into temptation.

THE TEMPTATION OF CHRIST
(MATTHEW 4)

What does this mean?

Answer: God tempts no one. We pray in this petition that God would guard and keep us so that the devil, the world, and our sinful nature may not deceive us or mislead us into false belief, despair, and other great shame and vice. Although we are attacked by these things, we pray that we may finally overcome them and win the victory.

The Seventh Petition

But deliver us from evil.
But deliver us from evil.

What does this mean?

Answer: We pray in this petition, in summary, that our Father in heaven would rescue us from every evil of body and soul, possessions and reputation, and finally, when our last hour comes, give us a blessed end, and graciously take us from this valley of sorrow to Himself in heaven.

CHRIST HEALS THE CANAANITE WOMAN'S DAUGHTER (MATTHEW 15)

For Thine is the kingdom and the power and the glory forever and ever.* Amen.
For the kingdom, the power, and the glory are Yours now and forever. Amen.*

What does this mean?

Answer: This means that I should be certain that these petitions are pleasing to our Father in heaven, and are heard by Him; for He Himself has commanded us to pray in this way and has promised to hear us. Amen, amen means "yes, yes, it shall be so."

*These words were not in Luther's Small Catechism.

IV. THE SACRAMENT OF HOLY BAPTISM

AS THE HEAD OF THE FAMILY SHOULD TEACH IT IN A SIMPLE WAY TO HIS HOUSEHOLD

THE BAPTISM OF CHRIST (MATTHEW 3)

First

What is Baptism?

Answer: Baptism is not just plain water, but it is the water included in God's command and combined with God's word.

Which is that word of God?

Answer: Christ our Lord says in the last chapter of Matthew: "Therefore go and make disciples of all nations, baptizing them in the name of the Father and of the Son and of the Holy Spirit." (Matthew 28:19)

Second

What benefits does Baptism give?

Answer: It works forgiveness of sins, rescues from death and the devil, and gives eternal salvation to all who believe this, as the words and promises of God declare.

Which are these words and promises of God?

Answer: Christ our Lord says in the last chapter of Mark: "Whoever believes and is baptized will be saved, but whoever does not believe will be condemned." (Mark 16:16)

CHRIST WITH THE LITTLE CHILDREN (LUKE 18)

Third

How can water do such great things?

Answer: Certainly not just water, but the word of God in and with the water does these things, along with the faith which trusts this word of God in the water. For without God's word the water is plain water and no Baptism. But with the word of God it is a Baptism, that is, a life-giving water, rich in grace, and a washing of the new birth in the Holy Spirit, as St. Paul says in Titus, chapter three:

"He saved us through the washing of rebirth and renewal by the Holy Spirit, whom He poured out on us generously through Jesus Christ our Savior, so that, having been justified by His grace, we might become heirs having the hope of eternal life. This is a trustworthy saying." (Titus 3:5–8)

Fourth

What does such baptizing with water indicate?

Answer: It indicates that the Old Adam in us should by daily contrition and repentance be drowned and die with all sins and evil desires, and that a new man should daily emerge and arise to live before God in righteousness and purity forever.

Where is this written?

Answer: St. Paul writes in Romans chapter six: "We were therefore buried with Him through baptism into death in order that, just as Christ was raised from the dead through the glory of the Father, we too may live a new life." (Romans 6:4)

V. CONFESSION

HOW CHRISTIANS SHOULD BE TAUGHT TO CONFESS

What is Confession?

Answer: Confession has two parts.

First, that we confess our sins, and

second, that we receive absolution, that is, forgiveness, from the pastor as from God Himself, not doubting, but firmly believing that by it our sins are forgiven before God in heaven.

CONFESSION AND ABSOLUTION (JOHN 21)

What sins should we confess?

Answer: Before God we should plead guilty of all sins, even those we are not aware of, as we do in the Lord's Prayer; but before the pastor we should confess only those sins which we know and feel in our hearts.

Which are these?

Answer: Consider your place in life according to the Ten Commandments: Are you a father, mother, son, daughter, husband, wife, or worker? Have you been disobedient, unfaithful, or lazy? Have you been hot-tempered, rude, or quarrelsome? Have you hurt someone by your words or deeds? Have you stolen, been negligent, wasted anything, or done any harm?

A Short Form of Confession

[Luther intended the following form to serve only as an example of private confession for Christians of his time. For a contemporary form of individual confession, see *Lutheran Service Book*, pp. 292–93.]

The penitent says:

Dear confessor, I ask you please to hear my confession and to pronounce forgiveness in order to fulfill God's will.

I, a poor sinner, plead guilty before God of all sins. In particular I confess before you that as a servant, maid, etc., I, sad to say, serve my master unfaithfully, for in this and that I have not done what I was told to do. I have made him angry and caused him to curse. I have been negligent and allowed damage to be done. I have also been offensive in words and deeds. I have quarreled with my peers. I have grumbled about the lady of the house and cursed her. I am sorry for all of this and I ask for grace. I want to do better.

A master or lady of the house may say:

In particular I confess before you that I have not faithfully guided my children, servants, and wife to the glory of God. I have cursed. I have set a bad example by indecent words and deeds. I have hurt my neighbor and spoken evil of him. I have overcharged, sold inferior merchandise, and given less than was paid for.

[Let the penitent confess whatever else he has done against God's commandments and his own position.]

If, however, someone does not find himself burdened with these or greater sins, he should not trouble himself or search for or invent other sins, and thereby make confession a torture. Instead, he should mention one or two that he knows: In particular I confess that I have cursed; I have used improper words; I have neglected this or that, etc. Let that be enough.

But if you know of none at all (which hardly seems possible), then mention none in particular, but receive the forgiveness upon the general confession which you make to God before the confessor.

Then the confessor shall say:

God be merciful to you and strengthen your faith. Amen.

Furthermore:

Do you believe that my forgiveness is God's forgiveness?

Yes, dear confessor.

Then let him say:

Let it be done for you as you believe. And I, by the command of our Lord Jesus Christ, forgive you your sins in the name of the Father and of the Son and of the Holy Spirit. Amen. Go in peace.

A confessor will know additional passages with which to comfort and to strengthen the faith of those who have great burdens of conscience or are sorrowful and distressed.

This is intended only as a general form of confession.

*What is the Office of the Keys?**

The Office of the Keys is that special authority which Christ has given to His church on earth to forgive the sins of repentant sinners, but to withhold forgiveness from the unrepentant as long as they do not repent.

*Where is this written?**

This is what St. John the Evangelist writes in chapter twenty: The Lord Jesus breathed on His disciples and said, "Receive the Holy Spirit. If you forgive anyone his sins, they are forgiven; if you do not forgive them, they are not forgiven." (John 20:22–23)

*What do you believe according to these words?**

I believe that when the called ministers of Christ deal with us by His divine command, in particular when they exclude openly unrepentant sinners from the Christian congregation and absolve those who repent of their sins and want to do better, this is just as valid and certain, even in heaven, as if Christ our dear Lord dealt with us Himself.

*This question may not have been composed by Luther himself but reflects his teaching and was included in editions of the catechism during his lifetime.

VI. THE SACRAMENT OF THE ALTAR

AS THE HEAD OF A FAMILY SHOULD TEACH IT IN A SIMPLE WAY TO HIS HOUSEHOLD

What is the Sacrament of the Altar?

Answer: It is the true body and blood of our Lord Jesus Christ under the bread and wine, instituted by Christ Himself for us Christians to eat and to drink.

Where is this written?

Answer: The holy Evangelists Matthew, Mark, Luke, and St. Paul, write:

Our Lord Jesus Christ, on the night when He was betrayed, took bread, and when He had given thanks, He broke it and gave it to the disciples and said: “Take, eat; this is My body, which is given for you. This do in remembrance of Me.”

In the same way also He took the cup after supper, and when He had given thanks, He gave it to them, saying, “Drink of it, all of you; this cup is the new testament in My blood, which is shed for you for the forgiveness of sins. This do, as often as you drink it, in remembrance of Me.”

What is the benefit of this eating and drinking?

Answer: These words, “Given and shed for you for the forgiveness of sins,” show us that in the Sacrament forgiveness of sins, life, and salvation are given us through these words. For where there is forgiveness of sins, there is also life and salvation.

How can bodily eating and drinking do such great things?

Answer: Certainly not just eating and drinking do these things, but the words written here: “Given and shed for you for the forgiveness of sins.” These words, along with the bodily eating and drinking, are the main thing in the Sacrament. Whoever believes these words has exactly what they say: “forgiveness of sins.”

Who receives this sacrament worthily?

Answer: Fasting and bodily preparation are certainly fine outward training. But that person is truly worthy and well prepared who has faith in these words: "Given and shed for you for the forgiveness of sins."

But anyone who does not believe these words or doubts them is unworthy and unprepared, for the words "for you" require all hearts to believe.

DAILY PRAYERS

HOW THE HEAD OF THE FAMILY SHOULD TEACH HIS HOUSEHOLD TO PRAY MORNING AND EVENING

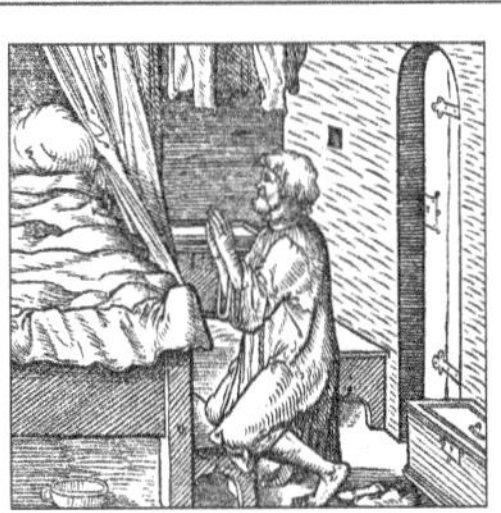

Morning Prayer

In the morning when you get up, make the sign of the holy cross and say:

In the name of the Father and of the ✠ Son and of the Holy Spirit. Amen.

Then, kneeling or standing, repeat the Creed and the Lord's Prayer. If you choose, you may also say this little prayer:

I thank You, my heavenly Father, through Jesus Christ, Your dear Son, that You have kept me this night from all harm and danger; and I pray that You would keep me this day also from sin and every evil, that all my doings and life may please You. For into Your hands I commend myself, my body and soul, and all things. Let Your holy angel be with me, that the evil foe may have no power over me. Amen.

Then go joyfully to your work, singing a hymn, like that of the Ten Commandments, or whatever your devotion may suggest.

Evening Prayer

In the evening when you go to bed, make the sign of the holy cross and say:

In the name of the Father and of the ✠ Son and of the Holy Spirit. Amen.

Then, kneeling or standing, repeat the Creed and the Lord's Prayer. If you choose, you may also say this little prayer:

I thank You, my heavenly Father, through Jesus Christ, Your dear Son, that You have graciously kept me this day; and I pray that You would forgive me all my sins where I have done wrong, and graciously keep me this night. For into Your hands I commend myself, my body and soul, and all things. Let Your holy angel be with me, that the evil foe may have no power over me. Amen.

Then go to sleep at once and in good cheer.

HOW THE HEAD OF THE FAMILY SHOULD TEACH HIS HOUSEHOLD TO ASK A BLESSING AND RETURN THANKS

Asking a Blessing

The children and members of the household shall go to the table reverently, fold their hands, and say:

The eyes of all look to You, [O LORD,] and You give them their food at the proper time. You open Your hand and satisfy the desires of every living thing. (Psalm 145:15–16)

Then shall be said the Lord's Prayer and the following:

Lord God, heavenly Father, bless us and these Your gifts which we receive from Your bountiful goodness, through Jesus Christ, our Lord. Amen.

Returning Thanks

Also, after eating, they shall, in like manner, reverently and with folded hands say:

Give thanks to the LORD, for He is good. His love endures forever. [He] gives food to every creature. He provides food for the cattle and for the young ravens when they call. His pleasure is not in the strength of the horse, nor His delight in the legs of a man; the LORD delights in those who fear Him, who put their hope in His unfailing love. (Psalm 136:1, 25; 147:9–11)

Then shall be said the Lord's Prayer and the following:

We thank You, Lord God, heavenly Father, for all Your benefits, through Jesus Christ, our Lord, who lives and reigns with You and the Holy Spirit forever and ever. Amen.

TABLE OF DUTIES

CERTAIN PASSAGES OF SCRIPTURE FOR VARIOUS HOLY ORDERS AND POSITIONS, ADMONISHING THEM ABOUT THEIR DUTIES AND RESPONSIBILITIES

To Bishops, Pastors, and Preachers

The overseer must be above reproach, the husband of but one wife, temperate, self-controlled, respectable, hospitable, able to teach, not given to drunkenness, not violent but gentle, not quarrelsome, not a lover of money. He must manage his own family well and see that his children obey him with proper respect. (1 Timothy 3:2–4)

He must not be a recent convert, or he may become conceited and fall under the same judgment as the devil. (1 Timothy 3:6)

He must hold firmly to the trustworthy message as it has been taught, so that he can encourage others by sound doctrine and refute those who oppose it. (Titus 1:9)

What the Hearers Owe Their Pastors

The Lord has commanded that those who preach the gospel should receive their living from the gospel. (1 Corinthians 9:14)

Anyone who receives instruction in the word must share all good things with his instructor. Do not be deceived: God cannot be mocked. A man reaps what he sows. (Galatians 6:6–7)

The elders who direct the affairs of the church well are worthy of double honor, especially those whose work is preaching and teaching. For the Scripture says, "Do not muzzle the ox while it is treading out the grain," and "The worker deserves his wages." (1 Timothy 5:17–18)

We ask you, brothers, to respect those who work hard among you, who are over you in the Lord and who admonish you. Hold them in the highest regard in love because of their work. Live in peace with each other. (1 Thessalonians 5:12–13)

Obey your leaders and submit to their authority. They keep watch over you as men who must give an account. Obey them so that their work will be a joy, not a burden, for that would be of no advantage to you. (Hebrews 13:17)

Of Civil Government

Everyone must submit himself to the governing authorities, for there is no authority except that which God has established. The authorities that exist have been established by God.

Consequently, he who rebels against the authority is rebelling against what God has instituted, and those who do so will bring judgment on themselves. For rulers hold no terror for those who do right, but for those who do wrong. Do you want to be free from fear of the one in authority? Then do what is right and he will commend you. For he is God's servant to do you good. But if you do wrong, be afraid, for he does not bear the sword for nothing. He is God's servant, an agent of wrath to bring punishment on the wrongdoer. (Romans 13:1–4)

Of Citizens

Give to Caesar what is Caesar's, and to God what is God's. (Matthew 22:21)

It is necessary to submit to the authorities, not only because of possible punishment but also because of conscience. This is also why you pay taxes, for the authorities are God's servants, who give their full time to governing. Give everyone what you owe him: If you owe taxes, pay taxes; if revenue, then revenue; if respect, then respect; if honor, then honor. (Romans 13:5–7)

I urge, then, first of all, that requests, prayers, intercession and thanksgiving be made for everyone—for kings and all those in authority, that we may live peaceful and quiet lives in all godliness and holiness. This is good, and pleases God our Savior. (1 Timothy 2:1–3)

Remind the people to be subject to rulers and authorities, to be obedient, to be ready to do whatever is good. (Titus 3:1)

Submit yourselves for the Lord's sake to every authority instituted among men: whether to the king, as the supreme authority, or to governors, who are sent by him to punish those who do wrong and to commend those who do right. (1 Peter 2:13–14)

To Husbands

Husbands, in the same way be considerate as you live with your wives, and treat them with respect as the weaker partner and as heirs with you of the gracious gift of life, so that nothing will hinder your prayers. (1 Peter 3:7)

Husbands, love your wives and do not be harsh will them. (Colossians 3:19)

To Wives

Wives, submit to your husbands as to the Lord. (Ephesians 5:22)

They were submissive to their own husbands, like Sarah, who obeyed Abraham and called him her master. You are her daughters if you do what is right and do not give way to fear. (1 Peter 3:5–6)

To Parents

Fathers, do not exasperate your children; instead, bring them up in the training and instruction of the Lord. (Ephesians 6:4)

To Children

Children, obey your parents in the Lord, for this is right. "Honor your father and your mother"—which is the first commandment with a promise—"that it may go well with you and that you may enjoy long life on the earth." (Ephesians 6:1–3)

To Workers of All Kinds

Slaves, obey your earthly masters with respect and fear, and with sincerity of heart, just as you would obey Christ. Obey them not only to win their favor when their eye is on you, but like slaves of Christ, doing the will of God from your heart. Serve wholeheartedly, as if you were serving the Lord, not men, because you know that the Lord will reward everyone for whatever good he does, whether he is slave or free. (Ephesians 6:5–8)

To Employers and Supervisors

Masters, treat your slaves in the same way. Do not threaten them, since you know that He who is both their Master and yours is in heaven, and there is no favoritism with Him. (Ephesians 6:9)

To Youth

Young men, in the same way be submissive to those who are older. All of you, clothe yourselves with humility toward one another, because, "God opposes the proud but gives grace to the humble." Humble yourselves, therefore, under God's mighty hand, that He may lift you up in due time. (1 Peter 5:5–6)

To Widows

The widow who is really in need and left all alone puts her hope in God and continues night and day to pray and to ask God for help. But the widow who lives for pleasure is dead even while she lives. (1 Timothy 5:5–6)

To Everyone

The commandments . . . are summed up in this one rule: "Love your neighbor as yourself." (Romans 13:9)

I urge . . . that requests, prayers, intercession

and thanksgiving be made for everyone." (1 Timothy 2:1)

Let each his lesson learn with care,
and all the household well shall fare.

Christian Questions with Their Answers

CHRISTIAN QUESTIONS WITH THEIR ANSWERS*

PREPARED BY DR. MARTIN LUTHER FOR THOSE WHO INTEND TO GO TO THE SACRAMENT

After confession and instruction in the Ten Commandments, the Creed, the Lord's Prayer, and the Sacraments of Baptism and the Lord's Supper, the pastor may ask, or Christians may ask themselves these questions:

1. ***Do you believe that you are a sinner?***

   Yes, I believe it. I am a sinner.

2. ***How do you know this?***

   From the Ten Commandments, which I have not kept.

3. ***Are you sorry for your sins?***

   Yes, I am sorry that I have sinned against God.

* The "Christian Questions with Their Answers," designating Luther as the author, first appeared in an edition of the Small Catechism in 1551.

4. *What have you deserved from God because of your sins?*

His wrath and displeasure, temporal death, and eternal damnation. See Romans 6:21, 23.

5. *Do you hope to be saved?*

Yes, that is my hope.

6. *In whom then do you trust?*

In my dear Lord Jesus Christ.

7. *Who is Christ?*

The Son of God, true God and man.

8. *How many Gods are there?*

Only one, but there are three persons: Father, Son, and Holy Spirit.

9. *What has Christ done for you that you trust in Him?*

He died for me and shed His blood for me on the cross for the forgiveness of sins.

10. *Did the Father also die for you?*

He did not. The Father is God only, as is the Holy Spirit; but the Son is both true God and true man. He died for me and shed His blood for me.

11. How do you know this?

From the holy Gospel, from the words instituting the Sacrament, and by His body and blood given me as a pledge in the Sacrament.

12. What are the words of institution?

Our Lord Jesus Christ, on the night when He was betrayed, took bread, and when He had given thanks, He broke it and gave it to the disciples and said: "Take eat; this is My body, which is given for you. This do in remembrance of Me."

In the same way also He took the cup after supper, and when He had given thanks, He gave it to them, saying: "Drink of it, all of you; this cup is the new testament in My blood, which is shed for you for the forgiveness of sins. This do, as often as you drink it, in remembrance of Me."

13. Do you believe, then, that the true body and blood of Christ are in the Sacrament?

Yes, I believe it.

14. What convinces you to believe this?

The word of Christ: Take, eat, this is My body; drink of it, all of you, this is My blood.

15. What should we do when we eat His body and drink His blood, and in this way receive His pledge?

We should remember and proclaim His death and the shedding of His blood, as He taught us: This do, as often as you drink it, in remembrance of Me.

16. Why should we remember and proclaim His death?

First, so that we may learn to believe that no creature could make satisfaction for our sins. Only Christ, true God and man, could do that. Second, so we may learn to be horrified by our sins, and to regard them as very serious. Third, so we may find joy and comfort in Christ alone, and through faith in Him be saved.

17. What motivated Christ to die and make full payment for your sins?

His great love for His Father and for me and other sinners, as it is written in John 14; Romans 5; Galatians 2; and Ephesians 5.

18. Finally, why do you wish to go to the Sacrament?

That I may learn to believe that Christ, out of great love, died for my sin, and also learn from Him to love God and my neighbor.

19. What should admonish and encourage a Christian to receive the Sacrament frequently?

First, both the command and the promise of Christ the Lord. Second, his own pressing need, because of which the command, encouragement, and promise are given.

20. But what should you do if you are not aware of this need and have no hunger and thirst for the Sacrament?

To such a person no better advice can be given than this:

first, he should touch his body to see if he still has flesh and blood. Then he should believe what the Scriptures say of it in Galatians 5 and Romans 7.

Second, he should look around to see whether he is still in the world, and remember that there will be no lack of sin and trouble, as the Scriptures say in John 15–16 and in 1 John 2 and 5.

Third, he will certainly have the devil also around him, who with his lying and murdering day and night will let him have no peace, within or without, as the Scriptures picture him in John 8 and 16; 1 Peter 5; Ephesians 6; and 2 Timothy 2.

Note: These questions and answers are no child's play, but are drawn up with great earnestness of purpose by the venerable and devout Dr. Luther for both young and old. Let each one pay attention and consider it a serious matter; for St. Paul writes to the Galatians in chapter six: "Do not be deceived: God cannot be mocked."

The Large Catechism

The Large Catechism

PREFACE

A Christian, profitable, and necessary preface, and faithful, serious encouragement from Dr. Martin Luther to all Christians, but especially to all pastors and preachers. They should daily exercise themselves in the catechism, which is a short summary and epitome of the entire Holy Scriptures. They should always teach the catechism.

1 We have no small reasons for constantly preaching the catechism and for both desiring and begging others to teach it. For sadly we see that many pastors and preachers are very negligent in this matter and slight both their office and this teaching. Some neglect the catechism because of great and high art ‹giving their mind, as they imagine, to much "higher" matters›. But others neglect it from sheer laziness and care for their bellies. They take no other stand in this business

than to act as pastors and preachers for their bellies' sake. They have nothing to do but to ‹spend and› consume their wages as long as they live, just as they used to do under the papacy.

They now have everything they are to preach and teach placed before them abundantly, clearly, and easily, in so many helpful books. These truly are "Sermons That Preach Themselves," "Sleep Soundly," "Be Prepared," and "Thesaurus," as they used to be called. Yet these preachers are not even godly and honest enough to buy these books or, even when they have them, to look at them or read them. Oh, they are completely shameful gluttons and servants of their own bellies. They are more fit to be swineherds and dog tenders than caretakers of souls and pastors. 2

These pastors are now released from the useless and burdensome babbling of the seven canonical hours of prayer. I wish that, instead of these, they would read each morning, noon, and evening only a page or two in the catechism, the prayer book, the New Testament, or something else in the Bible. They should pray the Lord's Prayer for themselves and their parishioners. Then they might respond with honor and thanks to the Gospel, by which they have been delivered from obvious burdens and troubles, and might 3

feel a little shame. For like pigs and dogs, they take nothing more from the Gospel than this lazy,
4 deadly, shameful, worldly freedom! The common people also respect the Gospel altogether too lightly, and we accomplish nothing special, even though we work diligently. What, then, would be achieved if we were as negligent and lazy as we were under the papacy?

5 To this laziness such preachers add the shameful vice and secret infection of security and contentment. In other words, many see the catechism as a poor, common teaching, which they can read through once and immediately understand. They can throw the book into a corner and be ashamed to read it again.

6 Yes, even among the nobility one may find some clowns and penny pinchers, who say (a) there is no longer any need for either pastors or preachers, (b) we have everything in books, and (c) everyone can easily learn it by himself. So they are happy to let the parishes rot and become empty. They let pastors and preachers worry and go hungry, just as crazy Germans are accustomed to do. For we Germans have such disgraceful people and must put up with them.

7 But for myself I say this: I am also a doctor and preacher; yes, as learned and experienced as all

THE CREATION; WOODCUT FROM THE FIRST ILLUSTRATED EDITION OF THE LARGE CATECHISM, 1530, WITTENBERG

the people who have such assumptions and contentment. Yet I act as a child who is being taught the catechism. Every morning—and whenever I have time—I read and say, word for word, the Ten Commandments, the Creed, the Lord's Prayer, the Psalms, and such. I must still read and study them daily. Yet I cannot master the cat-
8 echism as I wish. But I must remain a child and pupil of the catechism, and am glad to remain so. Yet these delicate, refined fellows would in one reading promptly become doctors above all doctors, know everything, and need nothing. Well, this, too, is a sure sign that they despise both their office and the souls of the people. Indeed, they even despise God and His Word. They do not have to fall. They have already fallen all too horribly. They need to become children and begin to learn their alphabet, which they imagine they have long outgrown [Mark 10:15].

9 Therefore, for God's sake I beg such lazy bellies or arrogant saints to be persuaded and believe that they are truly, truly not so learned or such great doctors as they imagine! They should never assume that they have finished learning the parts of the catechism or know it well enough in all points, even though they think that they know it ever so well. For even if they know and understand the catechism perfectly (which, however,

is impossible in this life), there are still many benefits and fruits to be gained, if it is daily read and practiced in thought and speech. For example, the Holy Spirit is present in such reading, repetition, and meditation. He bestows ever new and more light and devoutness. In this way the catechism is daily loved and appreciated better, as Christ promises in Matthew 18:20, "For where two or three are gathered in My name, there am I among them."

Besides, catechism study is a most effective 10
help against the devil, the world, the flesh, and all evil thoughts. It helps to be occupied with God's Word, to speak it, and meditate on it, just as the first Psalm declares people blessed who meditate on God's Law day and night (Psalm 1:2). Certainly you will not release a stronger incense or other repellant against the devil than to be engaged by God's commandments and words, and speak, sing, or think them [Colossians 3:16]. For this is indeed the true "holy water" and "holy sign" from which the devil runs and by which he may be driven away [James 4:7].

Now, for this reason alone you ought gladly 11
to read, speak, think, and use these things, even if you had no other profit and fruit from them than driving away the devil and evil thoughts by doing

so. For he cannot hear or endure God's Word. God's Word is not like some other silly babbling, like the story about Dietrich of Berne, for example. But as St. Paul says in Romans 1:16, it is "the power of God." Yes indeed, it is the power of God that gives the devil burning pain and strengthens, comforts, and helps us beyond measure.

12 And what need is there for more words? If I were to list all the profit and fruit God's Word produces, where would I get enough paper and time? The devil is called the master of a thousand arts. But what shall we call God's Word, which drives away and brings to nothing this master of a thousand arts with all his arts and power? The Word must indeed be the master of more than a
13 hundred thousand arts. And shall we easily despise such power, profit, strength, and fruit—we, especially, who claim to be pastors and preachers? If so, not only should we have nothing given us to eat, but we should also be driven out, baited with dogs, and pelted with dung. We not only need all this every day just as we need our daily bread, but we must also daily use it against the daily and unending attacks and lurking of the devil [1 Peter 5:8], the master of a thousand arts.

14 If these reasons were not enough to move us to read the catechism daily, we should feel

bound well enough by God's command alone. He solemnly commands in Deuteronomy 6:6–8 that we should always meditate on His precepts, sitting, walking, standing, lying down, and rising. We should have them before our eyes and in our hands as a constant mark and sign. Clearly He did not solemnly require and command this without a purpose. For He knows our danger and need, as well as the constant and furious assaults and temptations of devils. He wants to warn, equip, and preserve us against them, as with a good armor against their fiery darts [Ephesians 6:10–17] and with good medicine against their evil infection and temptation.

Oh, what mad, senseless fools are we! While 15
we must ever live and dwell among such mighty enemies as the devils, we still despise our weapons and defense [2 Corinthians 10:4], and we are too lazy to look at or think of them!

What else are such proud, arrogant saints 16
doing who are unwilling to read and study the catechism daily? They think they are much more learned than God Himself with all His saints, angels, prophets, apostles, and all Christians. God Himself is not ashamed to teach these things daily. He knows nothing better to teach. He always keeps teaching the same thing and does not

take up anything new or different. All the saints know nothing better or different to learn and cannot finish learning this. Are we not the finest of all fellows to imagine that if we have once read or heard the catechism, we know it all and have no further need to read and learn? Can we finish learning in one hour what God Himself cannot finish teaching? He is engaged in teaching this from the beginning to the end of the world. All prophets, together with all saints, have been busy learning it, have ever remained students, and must continue to be students.

17 It must be true that whoever knows the Ten Commandments perfectly must know all the Scriptures [Matthew 7:12]. So, in all matters and cases, he can advise, help, comfort, judge, and decide both spiritual and temporal matters. Such a person must be qualified to sit in judgment over all doctrines, estates, spirits, laws, and whatever
18 else is in the world [1 Corinthians 6:2–3]. And what, indeed, is the entire Book of Psalms but thoughts and exercises upon the First Commandment? Now I truly know that such lazy "bellies" and arrogant spirits do not understand a single psalm, much less the entire Holy Scriptures. Yet they pretend to know and despise the catechism, which is a short and brief summary of all the Holy Scriptures.

GOD GIVES THE COMMANDMENTS;
FROM 1530 LARGE CATECHISM

19 Therefore, I again beg all Christians—especially pastors and preachers—not to think of themselves as doctors too soon and imagine that they know everything. (For imagination, like unshrunk cloth, will fall far short of the measure.) Instead, they should daily exercise themselves well in these studies and constantly use them. Furthermore, they should guard with all care and diligence against the poisonous infection of contentment and vain imagination, but steadily keep on reading, teaching, learning, pondering, and meditating on the catechism. And they should not stop until they have tested and are sure that they have taught the devil to death, and have become more learned than God Himself and all His saints.

20 If they show such diligence, then I will promise them—and they shall also see—what fruit they will receive, and what excellent people God will make of them. So in due time they themselves will admit that the longer and the more they study the catechism, the less they know of it and the more they will find to learn. Only then, as hungry and thirsty men, will they truly relish what now they cannot stand because of great abundance and contentment. To this end may God grant His grace! Amen.

SHORT PREFACE OF DR. MARTIN LUTHER

This sermon is designed and undertaken to 1
be an instruction for children and the simple
folk. Therefore, in ancient times it was called in
Greek *catechism* (i.e., instruction for children).
It teaches what every Christian must know. So a 2
person who does not know this catechism could
not be counted as a Christian or be admitted to
any Sacrament, just as a mechanic who does not
understand the rules and customs of his trade is
expelled and considered incapable. Therefore, we 3
must have the young learn well and fluently the
parts of the catechism or instruction for children,
diligently exercise themselves in them, and keep
them busy with these parts.

Therefore, it is the duty of every father of a 4
family to question and examine his children and
servants at least once a week and see what they
know or are learning from the catechism. And if
they do not know the catechism, he should keep
them learning it faithfully. For I well remember 5
the time—indeed, even now it happens daily—
that one finds rude, old persons who knew nothing and still know nothing about these things. Yet

they go to Baptism and the Lord's Supper and use
everything belonging to Christians, even though
people who come to the Lord's Supper ought to
know more and have a fuller understanding of all
Christian doctrine than children and new schol-
6 ars. However, for the common people we are satisfied if they know the three "parts." These have
remained in Christendom from of old, though
little of them has been taught and used correctly
until both young and old (who are called Christians and wish to be so) are well trained in them
and familiar with them. These parts are the following:

FIRST

GOD'S TEN COMMANDMENTS

1 1. You shall have no other gods.

2 2. You shall not take the name of the Lord, your God, in vain.

3 3. You shall sanctify the holy day.

4 4. You shall honor your father and mother ‹that it may be well with you and you may live long upon the earth›.

5 5. You shall not murder.

6. You shall not commit adultery. 6

7. You shall not steal. 7

8. You shall not bear false witness against your 8
neighbor.

9. You shall not covet your neighbor's house. 9

10. You shall not covet your neighbor's wife, or his 10
manservant, or his maidservant, or his cattle, or anything that is his.

SECOND

THE CHIEF ARTICLES OF OUR FAITH

1. I believe in God, the Father Almighty, 11
maker of heaven and earth.

2. And in Jesus Christ, His only Son, our Lord, 12
who was conceived by the Holy Spirit, born of the virgin Mary, suffered under Pontius Pilate, was crucified, died and was buried. He descended into hell. The third day He rose again from the dead. He ascended into heaven and sits at the right hand of God the Father Almighty. From thence He will come to judge the living and the dead.

13 3. I believe in the Holy Spirit, the holy Christian Church, the communion of saints, the forgiveness of sins, the resurrection of the body, and the life everlasting. Amen.

14

THIRD

THE PRAYER, OR "OUR FATHER," WHICH CHRIST TAUGHT

Our Father who art in heaven.

1. Hallowed be Thy name.
2. Thy kingdom come.
3. Thy will be done on earth as it is in heaven.
4. Give us this day our daily bread.
5. And forgive us our trespasses as we forgive those who trespass against us.
6. And lead us not into temptation.
7. But deliver us from evil. [For Thine is the kingdom and the power and the glory forever and ever.] Amen.

15 These are the most necessary parts of Christian teaching that one should first learn to repeat
16 word for word. And our children should be used to reciting them daily when they rise in the morning, when they sit down to their meals, and when

they go to bed at night. And until they repeat them, they should not be given food or drink.
Likewise, every head of a household is bound to 17
do the same with his household, manservants, and maidservants. He should not keep them in his house if they do not know these things or
are unwilling to learn them. A person who is so 18
rude and unruly as to be unwilling to learn these things is not to be tolerated. For in these three parts, everything that we have in the Scriptures
is included in short, plain, and simple terms. For 19
the holy fathers or apostles (whoever first taught these things) have summarized the doctrine, life, wisdom, and art of Christians this way. These parts speak, teach, and are focused on them.

Now, when these three parts are understood, 20
a person must also know what to say about our Sacraments, which Christ Himself instituted: Baptism and the holy body and blood of Christ. They should know the texts that Matthew [28:19–20] and Mark [16:15–16] record at the close of their Gospels, when Christ said farewell to His disciples and sent them forth.

BAPTISM 21

Go therefore and make disciples of all nations, baptizing them in the name of the

Father and of the Son and of the Holy Spirit. [Matthew 28:19]

Whoever believes and is baptized will be saved, but whoever does not believe will be condemned. [Mark 16:16]

22 This is enough for a simple person to know from the Scriptures about Baptism. In like manner, in short, simple words, they should also know the text of St. Paul [1 Corinthians 11:23–26] about the other Sacrament.

THE SACRAMENT

23 Our Lord Jesus Christ, on the night He was betrayed, took bread, and when He had given thanks, He broke it and gave it to the disciples and said: "Take, eat; this is My body, which is given for you. This do in remembrance of Me."

In the same way also, He took the cup after supper, and when He had given thanks, He gave it to them, saying: "Drink of it, all of you; this is My blood of the new testament, which is shed for you for the forgiveness of sins. This do, as often as you drink it, in remembrance of Me."

Then we would have all together five whole 24
parts of Christian doctrine. These should be taught constantly and be required learning for children. You should hear them recited word for word. For you must not rely on the idea that the young people will learn and retain these things from the
sermon alone. When these parts have been well 25
learned, you may supplement and strengthen them by also setting before them some psalms or hymns, which have been composed on these parts of the catechism. Lead the young into the Scriptures this way, and make progress in them daily.

However, it is not enough for them to un- 26
derstand and recite these parts according to the words alone. The young people should also be made to attend the preaching, especially during the time that is devoted to the catechism. Then they may hear it explained and may learn to understand what every part contains, so that they can recite it the way they have heard it. Then, when asked, they may give a correct answer, so that preaching may not be useless and fruitless.
For the reason we exercise such diligence in 27
preaching the catechism often is so that it may be taught to our youth, not in a high and clever way, but briefly and with the greatest simplicity. In this way it will enter the mind easily and be fixed in the memory.

28 Therefore, we shall now take up the above-mentioned articles one by one, and in the plainest manner possible say as much as is necessary about them.

PART 1

THE FIRST COMMANDMENT

You shall have no other gods.

1 What this means: You shall have Me alone as your God. What is the meaning of this, and how is it to be understood? What does it mean to have
2 a god? Or, what is God? Answer: A god means that from which we are to expect all good and in which we are to take refuge in all distress. So, to have a God is nothing other than trusting and believing Him with the heart. I have often said that the confidence and faith of the heart alone
3 make both God and an idol. If your faith and trust is right, then your god is also true. On the other hand, if your trust is false and wrong, then you do not have the true God. For these two belong together, faith and God [Hebrews 11:6]. Now, I say that whatever you set your heart on and put your trust in is truly your god.

The purpose of this commandment is to 4
require true faith and trust of the heart, which
settles upon the only true God and clings to Him
alone. It is like saying, "See to it that you let Me
alone be your God, and never seek another." In
other words, "Whatever you lack of good things,
expect it from Me. Look to Me for it. And whenever you suffer misfortune and distress, crawl and
cling to Me. I, yes, I, will give you enough and
help you out of every need. Only do not let your
heart cleave to or rest on any other."

This point I must unfold more clearly. It may 5
be understood and seen through ordinary, coun-
terexamples. Many a person thinks that he has
God and everything in abundance when he has
money and possessions. He trusts in them and
boasts about them with such firmness and assurance as to care for no one. Such a person has a 6
god by the name of "Mammon" (i.e., money and
possessions; [Matthew 6:24]), on which he sets all
his heart. This is the most common idol on earth. 7
He who has money and possessions feels secure
[Luke 12:16–21] and is joyful and undismayed as
though he were sitting in the midst of Paradise.
On the other hand, he who has no money doubts 8
and is despondent, as though he knew of no God.
For very few people can be found who are of 9

good cheer and who neither mourn nor complain if they lack Mammon. This care and desire for money sticks and clings to our nature, right up to the grave.

10 So, too, whoever trusts and boasts that he has great skill, prudence, power, favor, friendship, and honor also has a god. But it is not the true and only God. This truth reappears when you notice how arrogant, secure, and proud people are because of such possessions, and how despondent they are when the possessions no longer exist or are withdrawn. Therefore, I repeat that the chief explanation of this point is that to "have a god" is to have something in which the heart entirely trusts.

11 Besides, consider our blindness, which we have been practicing and doing under the papacy up until now. If anyone had a toothache, he fasted and honored St. Apollonia. If he was afraid of fire, he chose St. Lawrence as his helper. If he dreaded bubonic plague, he made a vow to St. Sebastian or Rochio. There were a countless number of such abominations, where everyone chose his own saint, worshiped him, and called to him for help
12 in distress. Here belong such people as sorcerers and magicians, whose idolatry is most great [Deuteronomy 18:9–12]. They make a deal with

the devil, in order that he may give them plenty of money or help them in love affairs, preserve their cattle, restore to them lost possessions, and so forth. For all such people place their heart and trust elsewhere than in the true God. They look to Him for nothing good, nor do they seek good from Him.

So you can easily understand what and how 13
much this commandment requires. A person's
entire heart and all his confidence must be placed
in God alone and in no one else. For to "have"
God, you can easily see, is not to take hold of
Him with our hands or to put Him in a bag ‹like
money› or to lock Him in a chest ‹like silver ves-
sels›. Instead, to "have" Him means that the heart 14
takes hold of Him and clings to Him. To cling to 15
Him with the heart is nothing else than to trust in
Him entirely. For this reason God wishes to turn
us away from everything else that exists outside of
Him and to draw us to Himself [John 6:44]. For
He is the only eternal good [Matthew 19:17]. It
is as though He would say, "Whatever you have
previously sought from the saints, or for whatever
things you have trusted in money or anything
else, expect it all from Me. Think of Me as the one
who will help you and pour out upon you richly
all good things."

16 See, here you have the meaning of the true honor and worship of God, which pleases God, and which He commands under penalty of eternal wrath. The heart knows no other comfort or confidence than in Him. It must not allow itself to be torn from Him. But, for Him, it must risk and
17 disregard everything upon earth. On the other hand, you can easily see and sense how the world practices only false worship and idolatry. For no people have ever been so corrupt that they did not begin and continue some divine worship. Everyone has set up as his special god whatever he looked to for blessings, help, and comfort.

18 For example, the heathen who put their trust in power and dominion elevated Jupiter as the supreme god. Others, who were bent on riches, happiness, or pleasure, and a life of ease, elevated Hercules, Mercury, Venus, or other gods. Pregnant women elevated Diana or Lucina, and so on. So everyone made his god that interest to which his heart was inclined. So even in the mind of the heathen to have a god means to trust and
19 believe. But their error is this: their trust is false and wrong. For their trust is not placed in the only God, beside whom there is truly no God in
20 heaven or upon earth [Isaiah 44:6]. Therefore, the heathen really make their self-invented notions

and dreams of God an idol. Ultimately, they put
their trust in that which is nothing. So it is with 21
all idolatry. For it happens not merely by erecting
an image and worshiping it, but rather it happens
in the heart. For the heart stands gaping at something else. It seeks help and consolation from
creatures, saints, or devils. It neither cares for
God, nor looks to Him for anything better than to
believe that He is willing to help. The heart does
not believe that whatever good it experiences
comes from God [James 1:17].

Beside this, there is also a false worship and 22
extreme idolatry, which we have practiced up to
now. This is also still common in the world. All
churchly orders are founded on it. It concerns the
conscience alone, which seeks help, consolation,
and salvation in its own works. This conscience
imagines it can wrestle heaven away from God
and thinks about how many requests it has made,
how often it has fasted, celebrated Mass, and so
on. Upon such things it depends and boasts, as
though unwilling to receive anything from God
as a gift. For it wants to earn or merit heaven with
abundant works. The conscience acts as though
God must serve us and is our debtor, and we are
His liege lords. What is this but reducing God to 23
an idol—indeed, an apple-god—and elevating

and regarding ourselves as God? But this point is a little too clever and is not for young pupils.

24 Let the following point be made to the simple; then they may well note and remember the meaning of this commandment: We are to trust in God alone and look to Him and expect from Him nothing but good, as from one who gives us body, life, food, drink, nourishment, health, protection, peace, and all necessaries of both temporal and eternal things. He also preserves us from misfortune. And if any evil befall us, He delivers and rescues us. So it is God alone (as has been said well enough) from whom we receive all good
25 and by whom we are delivered from all evil. So, I think, we Germans from ancient times name *God* (more elegantly and appropriately than any other language) from the word *Good*. It is as though He were an eternal fountain that gushes forth abundantly nothing but what is good. And from that fountain flows forth all that is and is called good.

26 Even though we experience much good from other people, whatever we receive by God's command or arrangement is all received from God. For our parents and all rulers and everyone else, with respect to his neighbor, have received from God the command that they should do us all kinds of good. So we receive these blessings

not from them, but through them, from God. For creatures are only the hands, channels, and means by which God gives all things. So He gives to the mother breasts and milk to offer to her child, and He gives corn and all kinds of produce from the earth for nourishment [Psalm 104:27–28; 147:8–9]. None of these blessings could be produced by any creature of itself.

So no one should expect to take or give any- 27
thing except what God has commanded. Then it may be acknowledged as God's gift, and thanks may be rendered to Him for it, as this commandment requires. For this reason also, the ways we receive good gifts through creatures are not to be rejected. Nor should we arrogantly seek other ways and means than what God has commanded. For that would not be receiving from God, but seeking for ourselves.

Let everyone, then, see to it that he values this 28
commandment great and high above all things. Do not regard it as a joke! Ask and examine your heart diligently [2 Corinthians 13:5], and you will find out whether it clings to God alone or not. If you have a heart that can expect of Him nothing but what is good—especially in need and distress—and a heart that also renounces and forsakes everything that is not God, then

you have the only true God. If, on the contrary, your heart clings to anything else from which it expects more good and help than from God, and if your heart does not take refuge in Him but flees from Him when in trouble, then you have an idol, another god.

29 God will not have this commandment thrown to the winds. He will most strictly enforce it. In order that this may be known He has added (a) a terrible threat and (b) a beautiful, comforting promise. This promise is also to be taught and impressed upon young people [Deuteronomy 6:7], that they may take it to heart and hold it.

‹Explanation of the Appendix to the First Commandment›

30 I the Lord your God am a jealous God, visiting the iniquity of the fathers on the children to the third and the fourth generation of those who hate Me, but showing steadfast love to thousands of those who love Me and keep My commandments. [Exodus 20:5–6]

31 These words relate to all the commandments (as we shall learn later). But they are joined to this chief commandment because it is most important that people get their thinking straight first. For where the head is right, the whole life

must be right, and vice versa. Learn, therefore, 32
from these words how angry God is with those
who trust in anything but Him. And again, learn
how good and gracious He is to those who trust
and believe in Him alone with their whole heart
[Deuteronomy 6:5]. His anger does not stop until
the fourth generation of those who hate Him. He 33
says this so you will not live in such security and
commit yourself to chance, like people with brute
hearts who think that it makes no great difference
how they live. On the other hand, His blessing
and goodness reach many thousands. He is a 34
God who will not overlook that people turn from
Him. He will not stop being angry until the fourth
generation, even until they are utterly exterminated. Therefore, He is to be feared and not to be
despised [Deuteronomy 10:20].

He has also made this known in all history, as 35
the Scriptures abundantly show and daily experience still teaches. For from the beginning He has
utterly uprooted all idolatry. Because of idolatry,
He has uprooted both heathen people and Jewish
people. To this day He overthrows all false worship, so that all who remain therein must finally
perish [2 Chronicles 7:19–20]. Proud, power- 36
ful, and rich men of the world ‹Sardanapalians
and Phalarides, who surpass even the Persians

in wealth› are still to be found. They boast defiantly of their Mammon. They utterly disregard whether God is angry at them or smiles on them. They dare to withstand His wrath, yet they shall not succeed. Before they are aware of it, they shall be wrecked, with all in which they trusted. All others have perished like this who have thought themselves more secure or powerful.

37 Such hard heads imagine that God overlooks and allows them to rest in security, or that He is entirely ignorant or cares nothing about such matters. Therefore, God must deal a smashing blow and punish them, so that He cannot forget their sin unto their children's children. In that way, everyone may take note and see that this is
38 no joke to Him. These are the people He means when He says, "those who hate Me" [Exodus 20:5], i.e., those who persist in their defiance and pride. Whatever is preached or said to them, they will not listen. When they are rebuked, in order that they may learn to know themselves and make amends before the punishment begins, they become mad and foolish. They rightly deserve wrath, as we see daily in bishops and princes now.

39 But as terrible as these threatenings are, so much more powerful is the consolation in the promise. For those who cling to God alone

should be sure that He will show them mercy. In
other words, He will show them pure goodness
and blessing, not only for themselves, but also to
their children and their children's children, even
to the thousandth generation and beyond that.
This ought certainly to move and impel us to risk 40
our hearts in all confidence with God [Hebrews
4:16; 10:19–23], if we wish all temporal and eternal good. For the supreme Majesty makes such
outstanding offers and presents such heartfelt
encouragements and such rich promises.

Therefore, let everyone seriously take this pas- 41
sage to heart, lest it be regarded as though a man had spoken it. For you it is a question of eternal blessing, happiness, and salvation, or of eternal wrath, misery, and woe. What more would you have or desire than God so kindly promising to be yours with every blessing and to protect and help you in all need?

But unfortunately, here is the failure: the 42
world believes none of this, nor regards it as God's Word. For the world sees that those who trust in God and not in Mammon suffer care and want, and that the devil opposes and resists them. They don't have money or favor or honor, and besides, can scarcely support life. On the other hand, those who serve Mammon have power,

favor, honor, possessions, and every comfort in the eyes of the world. For this reason, these words must be understood to speak against the appearance of such things. And we must consider that they do not lie or deceive, but must come true.

43 Reflect for yourself or investigate and tell me: Those who have used all their care and diligence to gather great possessions and wealth, what have they finally gained? You will find that they have wasted their toil and labor, or even though they have amassed great treasures, they have been dispersed and scattered [Luke 12:16–21]. So they themselves have never found happiness in their wealth, and afterward, it never reached the third generation.

44 You will find plenty of examples in all histories, also in the memory of aged and experienced people. Just watch and ponder them.

45 Saul was a great king, chosen by God, and a godly man. But when he was established on his throne, he let his heart wander from God and put his trust in his crown and power [1 Samuel 9–13]. Then he had to perish with all he had, so that not even his children remained [1 Samuel 31].

46 David, on the other hand, was a poor, despised man, hunted down and chased, so that

he did not feel his life was secure anywhere [1 Samuel 19–29]. Yet, he had to survive in spite of Saul, and become king [2 Samuel 2]. For these words of the promise had to abide and come true, since God cannot lie or deceive [Titus 1:2]. Just let not the devil and the world deceive you with their show, which indeed remains for a time, but finally is nothing.

Let us, then, learn well the First Command- 47
ment, that we may see how God will tolerate no overconfidence nor any trust in any other object. We will see how He requires nothing greater from us than confidence from the heart for everything good. Then we may live right and straightforward and use all the blessings that God gives, just as a shoemaker uses his needle, awl, and thread for work and then lays them aside. Or we may behave like a traveler using an inn, food, and bed only to meet his present need. Each person may do this in his calling, according to God's order, and without allowing any of these things to be his lord or idol.
This is enough about the First Commandment, 48
which we have had to explain at length, since it is of chief importance. For, as said earlier, where the heart is rightly set toward God [Deuteronomy 32:46] and this commandment is observed, all the other commandments follow.

THE SECOND COMMANDMENT

49 **You shall not take the name of the Lord, your God, in vain.**

50 The First Commandment has instructed the heart and taught the faith. This commandment now leads us forward and directs the mouth and tongue to God. For the first things that spring from the heart and show themselves are words [Matthew 12:34]. I have taught above how to answer the question "What does it mean to have a god?" Now you must simply learn to understand the meaning of this commandment and all the commandments, and to apply it to yourself.

51 If someone now asks, "How do you understand the Second Commandment?" or "What is meant by taking God's name in vain, or misusing God's name?" answer briefly in this way: "It means misusing God's name when we call upon the Lord God—no matter how—in order to deceive or do wrong of any kind." Therefore, this commandment makes this point: God's name must not be appealed to falsely, or taken upon the lips, while the heart knows well enough—or should know—that the truth of the matter is different. This is what happens with people who take

oaths in court, where one side lies against the other. For God's name cannot be misused worse 52 than for the support of falsehood and deceit. Let this remain the exact German and simplest meaning of this commandment.

From this everyone can easily see when and 53 in how many ways God's name is misused, although it is impossible to list all its misuses. But, to explain this in a few words, all misuse of the divine name happens first in worldly business and in matters that concern money, possessions, and honor. This applies publicly in court, in the market, or wherever else people make false oaths in God's name or pledge their souls in any matter. This is especially common in marriage affairs, where two go and secretly get engaged to one another, and afterward, break their engagement.

But the greatest abuse occurs in spiritual mat- 54 ters. These have to do with the conscience, when false preachers rise up and offer their lying vanities as God's Word [Jonah 2:8].

Look, all this is dressing up one's self with 55 God's name, or making a pretty show, or claiming to be right. This is true whether it happens in common, worldly business or in higher, refined matters of faith and doctrine. Blasphemers also belong with the liars. I mean not just the most ordinary blasphemers, well known to everyone, who disgrace God's name without fear. (These are not for us to discipline, but for the hangman.) I also mean those who publicly disgrace the truth and God's Word and hand it over to the devil. There is now no need to speak about this further.

56 Here, then, let us learn and take to heart the great importance of this commandment. Then, with all diligence, we may guard against and dread every misuse of the holy name as the greatest sin that can be committed outwardly. For to lie and to deceive is in itself a great sin. But such a sin gets even worse when we try to justify our lie and seek to confirm it by calling on God's name and using His name as a cloak for shame [1 Peter 2:16], so that from a single lie a double lie results—no, many lies.

57 For this reason, too, God has added a solemn threat to this commandment, "For the Lord will not hold him guiltless who takes His name in vain" [Exodus 20:7]. This means that this sin shall not be pardoned for anyone or go unpunished. For just as He will not fail to avenge if anyone turns his heart from Him, so He will also not let
58 His name be used to dress up a lie. Now unfortunately, this sin is a common plague in all the

world. There are so few people who do not use God's name for purposes of lying and all wickedness in contrast to those who trust in God alone with their heart.

By nature we all have within us this beauti- 59
ful virtue, that whoever has committed a wrong would like to cover up and adorn his disgrace, so that no one may see it or know it. No one is so bold as to boast to all the world of the wickedness he has done. All wish to act by stealth and without anyone being aware of what they do. So, if anyone is caught sinning, God's name is dragged into the affair and must make the wickedness look like
godliness, and the shame like honor. This is the 60
common way of the world, which has covered all lands like a great flood. So we get what we seek and deserve as our reward: epidemics, wars, famines, raging fires, floods, wayward wives, children, servants, and all sorts of filth. Where else should so much misery come from? It is still a great mercy that the earth bears and supports us [Numbers 16:28–50].

Therefore, above all things, our young people 61
should have this Second Commandment earnestly pressed upon them [Deuteronomy 6:7]. They should be trained to hold this and the First Commandment in high regard. And whenever they

sin, we must at once be after them with the rod [Proverbs 13:24]. We must hold the commandment before them, and constantly teach it, so that we bring them up not only with punishment, but also in reverence and fear of God [Ephesians 6:4].

62 Now you understand what it means to take God's name in vain. In sum it means (a) to use His name simply for purposes of falsehood, (b) to assert in God's name something that is not true, or (c) to curse, swear, use spells, and, in short, to practice whatever wickedness one may.

63 Besides this you must also know how to use God's name rightly. For when He says, "You shall not take the name of the Lord, your God, in vain," He wants us to understand at the same time that His name is to be used properly. For His name has been revealed and given to us so that it may
64 be of constant use and profit. So it is natural to conclude that since this commandment forbids using the holy name for falsehood or wickedness, we are, on the other hand, commanded to use His name for truth and for all good, like when someone takes an oath truthfully when it is needed and it is demanded [Numbers 30:2]. This commandment also applies to right teaching and to calling on His name in trouble or praising and thanking Him in prosperity, and so on. All

of this is summed up and commanded in Psalm 50:15, "Call upon Me in the day of trouble; I will deliver you, and you shall glorify Me." For all this is bringing God's name into the service of truth and using it in a blessed way. In this way His name is hallowed, as we pray in the Lord's Prayer [Matthew 6:9].

Now you have the sum of the entire com- 65
mandment explained. With this understanding,
the question that has troubled many teachers has
been easily solved: "Why is swearing prohibited
in the Gospel, and yet Christ, St. Paul, and other
saints often swore?" [Matthew 5:33–37; 26:29;
Acts 21:20–26]. The explanation is briefly this: 66
We are not to swear in support of evil, that is, to
support falsehood, or to swear when there is no
need or use. But we should swear for the support
of good and the advantage of our neighbor. For
such swearing is truly a good work, by which
God is praised, truth and right are established,
falsehood is refuted, peace is made among men,
obedience is rendered, and quarrels are settled.
For in this way God Himself intervenes and separates right and wrong, good and evil. If one party 67
swears falsely, he lives under this judgment: he
shall not escape punishment. Even if this judgment is delayed a long time, he shall not succeed.

So everything he may gain from his falsehood will
68 slip out of his hands, and he will never enjoy it. I have seen this in the case of many who perjured themselves in their wedding vows. They have never had a happy hour or a healthful day, and so perished miserably in body, soul, and possessions.

69 Therefore, I advise and exhort as before that with warning and threatening, restraint and punishment, the children should be trained early to shun falsehood. They should especially avoid the use of God's name to support falsehood. For where children are allowed to do as they please, no good will result. This is clear even now. The world is worse than it has ever been, and there is no government, no obedience, no loyalty, no faith, but only daring, unbridled people. No teaching or reproof helps them. All this is God's wrath and punishment for such lewd contempt of this commandment.

70 On the other hand, children should be constantly urged and moved to honor God's name and to have it always upon their lips for everything that may happen to them or come to their notice [Psalm 8:2; 34:1; Matthew 21:16; Hebrews 13:15]. For that is the true honor of His name, to look to it and call upon it for all consolation

[Psalm 66:2; 105:1]. Then—as we have heard in the First Commandment—the heart by faith gives God the honor due Him first. Afterward, the lips give Him honor by confession.

This is also a blessed and useful habit and very 71
effective against the devil. He is ever around us and lies in wait to bring us into sin and shame, disaster and trouble [2 Timothy 2:26]. But he hates to hear God's name and cannot remain long where it is spoken and called upon from the
heart. Indeed, many terrible and shocking disas- 72
ters would fall upon us if God did not preserve us by our calling upon His name. I have tried it myself. I learned by experience that often sudden great suffering was immediately averted and removed by calling on God. To confuse the devil, I say, we should always have this holy name in our mouth, so that the devil may not be able to injure us as he wishes.

It is also useful that we form the habit of daily 73
commending ourselves to God [Psalm 31:5], with soul and body, wife, children, servants, and all that we have, against every need that may arise. So also the blessing and thanksgiving at meals [Mark 8:6] and other prayers, morning and evening, have begun and remained in use [Exodus
29:38–43]. Likewise, children should continue to 74

cross themselves when anything monstrous or terrible is seen or heard. They can shout, "Lord God, protect us!" "Help, dear Lord Jesus!" and such. Also, if anyone meets with unexpected good fortune, however trivial, he says, "God be praised and thanked!" or "God has bestowed this on me!" and so on, just as the children used to learn to fast and pray to St. Nicholas and other saints before. This would be more pleasing and acceptable to God than all monasticism and Carthusian acts of holiness.

75 Look, we could train our youth this way [Proverbs 22:6], in a childlike way and playfully in the fear and honor of God. Then the First and Second Commandments might be well kept and in constant practice. Then some good might take root, spring up, and bear fruit. People would grow up whom an entire land might relish and
76 enjoy. In addition, this would be the true way to bring up children well as long as they could be trained with kindness and delight. For children who must be forced with rods and blows will not develop into a good generation. At best they will remain godly under such treatment only as long as the rod is upon their backs [Proverbs 10:13].

77 But ‹teaching the commandments in a childlike and playful way› spreads its roots in the heart

so that children fear God more than rods and clubs. This I say with such simplicity for the sake of the young, that it may penetrate their minds. For we are preaching to children, so we must also talk like them. In this way we would prevent the abuse of the divine name and teach the right use. This should happen not only in words, but also in practice and life. Then we may know God is well pleased with this and will as richly reward good use of His name as He will terribly punish the abuse.

THE THIRD COMMANDMENT

You shall sanctify the holy day. 78

The word *holiday* is used for the Hebrew word 79
sabbath, which properly means "to rest," that is,
to cease from labor. Therefore, we usually say,
"to stop working." Or "Sanctify the Sabbath."
Now, in the Old Testament, God set apart the 80
seventh day and appointed it for rest [Genesis
2:3]. He commanded that it should be regarded
as holy above all other days. This commandment
was given only to the Jewish people for this outward obedience, that they should stop toilsome work and rest. In that way both man and beast might recover and not be weakened by endless

81 labor [Exodus 20:8–11]. Later, the Jewish people restricted the Sabbath too closely and greatly abused it. They defamed Christ and could not endure in Him the same works that they themselves would do on that day, as we read in the Gospel [Matthew 12:11]. They acted as though the commandment were fulfilled by doing no manual work whatsoever. This, however, was not the meaning. But, as we shall hear, they were supposed to sanctify the holy day or day of rest.

82 This commandment, therefore, in its literal sense, does not apply to us Christians. It is entirely an outward matter, like other ordinances of the Old Testament. The ordinances were attached to particular customs, persons, times, and places, but now they have been made matters of freedom through Christ [Colossians 2:16–17].

83 The simpleminded need to grasp a Christian meaning about what God requires in this commandment. Note that we don't keep holy days for the sake of intelligent and learned Christians. (They have no need of holy days.) We keep them first of all for bodily causes and necessities, which nature teaches and requires. We keep them for the common people, manservants and maidservants, who have been attending to their work and trade the whole week. In this way they may withdraw in

order to rest for a day and be refreshed.

Second, and most especially, on this day of 84
rest (since we can get no other chance), we have the freedom and time to attend divine service. We come together to hear and use God's Word, and then to praise God, to sing and to pray [Colossians 3:16].

However, this keeping of the Sabbath, I point 85
out, is not restricted to a certain time, as with the Jewish people. It does not have to be just on this or that day. For in itself no one day is better than another [Romans 14:5–6]. Instead, this should be done daily. However, since the masses of people cannot attend every day, there must be at least one day in the week set apart. From ancient times Sunday ‹the Lord's Day› has been appointed for this purpose. So we also should continue to do the same, in order that everything may be done in an orderly way [1 Corinthians 14:40] and no one may create disorder by starting unnecessary practices.

This is the simple meaning of the command- 86
ment: People must have holidays. Therefore, such observances should be devoted to hearing God's Word so that the special function of this day of rest should be the ministry of the Word for the young and the mass of poor people [Nehemiah

8:2–3, 8]. Yet the resting should not be strictly understood to forbid any work that comes up, which cannot be avoided.

87 So when someone asks you, "What is meant by the commandment: You shall sanctify the holy day?" Answer like this, "To sanctify the holy day is the same as to keep it holy." "But what is meant by keeping it holy?" "Nothing else than to be occupied with holy words, works, and life." For the day needs no sanctification for itself. It has been created holy in itself. But God desires the day to be holy to you. Therefore, it becomes holy or unholy because of you, whether you are occupied on that day with things that are holy or unholy.

88 How, then, does such sanctification take place? Not like this: sitting behind the stove and doing no rough work, or adorning ourselves with a wreath and putting on our best clothes. But as said above, we occupy ourselves with God's Word and exercise ourselves in the Word.

89 Indeed, we Christians ought always to keep such a holy day and be occupied with nothing but holy things. This means we should daily be engaged with God's Word and carry it in our hearts and upon our lips [Psalm 119:11–13]. But as said above, since we do not always have free time, we must devote several hours a week for the

sake of the young, or at least a day for the sake of
the entire multitude, to being concerned about
this alone. We must especially teach the use of the
Ten Commandments, the Creed, and the Lord's
Prayer, and so direct our whole life and being
according to God's Word. At whatever time, 90
then, this is being observed and practiced, there
a true *holy day* is being kept. Other things shall
not be called a Christians' *holy day*. For, indeed,
non-Christians can also stop working and be idle,
just as the entire swarm of our Church workers
do. They stand daily in the churches, singing and
ringing bells, but they do not keep a holy day in
true holiness, because they do not preach or use
God's Word but teach and live contrary to it.

God's Word is the true "holy thing" [*Hei-* 91
ligtum; relic] above all holy things. Yes, it is the
only one we Christians know and have. Though
we had the bones of all the saints or all holy and
consecrated garments upon a heap, still that
would not help us at all. All that stuff is a dead
thing that can sanctify no one. But God's Word is
the treasure that sanctifies everything [1 Timothy
4:5]. By the Word even all the saints themselves
were sanctified [1 Corinthians 6:11]. Whenever 92
God's Word is taught, preached, heard, read, or
meditated upon, then the person, day, and work
are sanctified. This is not because of the outward

work, but because of the Word, which makes saints of us all. Therefore, I constantly say that all our life and work must be guided by God's Word, if it is to be God-pleasing or holy. Where this is done, this commandment is in force and being fulfilled.

93 On the contrary, any observance or work that is practiced without God's Word is unholy before God. This is true no matter how brilliantly a work may shine, even though it is covered with relics, such as the fictitious spiritual orders, which know nothing about God's Word and seek holiness in their own works.

94 Note, therefore, that the force and power of this commandment lies not in the resting, but in the sanctifying, so that a special *holy exercise* belongs to this day. For other works and occupations are not properly called holy exercises, unless the person is holy first. But here a work is to be done by which a person is himself made holy. This is done (as we have heard) only through God's Word. For this reason, particular places, times, persons, and the entire outward order of worship have been created and appointed, so that there may be order in public practice [1 Corinthians 14:40].

95 So much depends upon God's Word. Without

it, no holy day can be sanctified. Therefore, we must know that God insists upon a strict observance of this commandment and will punish all who despise His Word and are not willing to hear and learn it, especially at the time appointed for the purpose.

It is not only the people who greatly misuse 96
and desecrate the holy day who sin against this commandment (those who neglect to hear God's Word because of their greed or frivolity or lie in taverns and are dead drunk like swine). But even that other crowd sins. They listen to God's Word like it was any other trifle and only come to preaching because of custom. They go away again, and at the end of the year they know as
little of God's Word as at the beginning. Up to 97
this point the opinion prevailed that you had properly hallowed Sunday when you had heard a Mass or the Gospel read. But no one cared for God's Word, and no one taught it. Now that we have God's Word, we fail to correct the abuse. We allow ourselves to be preached to and admonished, but we do not listen seriously and carefully.

Know, therefore, that you must be concerned 98
not only about hearing, but also about learning and retaining God's Word in memory. Do not think that this is optional for you or of no great

importance. Think that it is God's commandment, who will require an account from you [Romans 14:12] about how you have heard, learned, and honored His Word.

99 Likewise, those fussy spirits are to be rebuked who, after they have heard a sermon or two, find hearing more sermons to be tedious and dull. They think that they know all that well enough and need no more instruction. For that is exactly the sin that was previously counted among mortal sins and is called *akadia* (i.e., apathy or satisfaction). This is a malignant, dangerous plague with which the devil bewitches and deceives the hearts of many so that he may surprise us and secretly take God's Word from us [Matthew 13:19].

100 Let me tell you this, even though you know God's Word perfectly and are already a master in all things: you are daily in the devil's kingdom [Colossians 1:13–14]. He ceases neither day nor night to sneak up on you and to kindle in your heart unbelief and wicked thoughts against these three commandments and all the commandments. Therefore, you must always have God's Word in your heart, upon your lips, and in your ears. But where the heart is idle and the Word does not make a sound, the devil breaks in and has done the damage before we are aware

[Matthew 13:24–30]. On the other hand, the 101
Word is so effective that whenever it is seriously
contemplated, heard, and used, it is bound never
to be without fruit [Isaiah 55:11; Mark 4:20]. It
always awakens new understanding, pleasure,
and devoutness and produces a pure heart and
pure thoughts [Philippians 4:8]. For these words
are not lazy or dead, but are creative, living words
[Hebrews 4:12]. And even though no other inter- 102
est or necessity moves us, this truth ought to urge
everyone to the Word, because thereby the devil
is put to flight and driven away [James 4:7]. Besides,
this commandment is fulfilled and this exercise
in the Word is more pleasing to God than
any work of hypocrisy, however brilliant.

THE FOURTH COMMANDMENT

So far we have learned the first three com- 103
mandments, which relate to God: (a) With our whole heart we trust in Him and fear and love Him throughout all our lives. (b) We do not misuse His holy name in support of falsehood or any bad work, but use it to praise God and for the profit and salvation of our neighbor and ourselves. (c) On holidays and when at rest we diligently use and encourage the use of God's Word, so that all our actions and our entire

life is guided by it. Now follow the other seven commandments, which relate to our neighbor. Among them is the first and greatest:

104 **You shall honor your father and your mother that it may be well with you and you may live long upon the earth.**

105 To the position of fatherhood and motherhood God has given special distinction above all positions that are beneath it: He does not simply command us to love our parents, but to honor them. Regarding our brothers, sisters, and neighbors in general, He commands nothing more than that we love them [Matthew 22:39; 1 John 3:14]. In this way He separates and distinguishes father and mother from all other persons upon
106 earth and places them at His side. For it is a far higher thing to honor someone than to love someone, because honor includes not only love, but also modesty, humility, and submission to a
107 majesty hidden in them. Honor requires not only that parents be addressed kindly and with reverence, but also that, both in the heart and with the body, we demonstrate that we value them very highly, and that, next to God, we regard them as the very highest. For someone we honor from the heart we must also truly regard as high and great.

We must, therefore, impress this truth upon 108
the young [Deuteronomy 6:7] that they should think of their parents as standing in God's place. They should remember that however lowly, poor, frail, and strange their parents may be, nevertheless, they are the father and the mother given to them by God. Parents are not to be deprived of their honor because of their conduct or their failings. Therefore, we are not to consider who they are or how they may be, but the will of God, who has created and ordained parenthood. In other respects people are, indeed, all equal in God's eyes. But among humans there must necessarily be this inequality and ordered difference. Therefore, God commands this order to be kept, that you obey me as your father [Matthew 5:48], and that I have the supremacy.

Learn, therefore, what is the honor towards 109
parents that this commandment requires. (a) They must be held in distinction and esteem above all things, as the most precious treasure on
earth. (b) In our words we must speak modestly 110
toward them [Proverbs 15:1]. Do not address them roughly, haughtily, and defiantly. But yield to them and be silent, even though they go too
far. (c) We must show them such honor also by 111
works, that is, with our body and possessions.

We must serve them, help them, and provide for them when they are old, sick, infirm, or poor. We must do all this not only gladly, but with humility and reverence, as doing it before God [Ephesians 6:6–7]. For the child who knows how to regard parents in his heart will not allow them to do without or hunger, but will place them above him and at his side and will share with them whatever he has and possesses.

112 Second, notice how great, good, and holy a work is assigned to children here. Unfortunately, this is utterly neglected and disregarded [Mark 7:10–13]. No one notices that God has commanded it or that it is a holy, divine Word and doctrine. For if it had been regarded as holy, everyone could have concluded that those who live according to these words must be holy people. There would have been no need to invent monasticism or spiritual orders. Every child would have abided by this commandment and could have directed his conscience to God and said, "If I am to do good and holy works, I know of none better than to give all honor and obedience to my parents, because God has Himself commanded
113 it. For what God commands must be much better and far nobler than everything that we may come up with ourselves. Since there is no higher

or better teacher to be found than God, there can certainly be no better teaching than what He provides. Now, He teaches fully what we should do if we wish to perform truly good works. By commanding such works, He shows that they please Him. If, then, it is God who commands this and does not know how to appoint anything better, I will never improve upon it."

Behold, in this way we would have had a godly child properly taught, reared in true blessedness, and kept at home in obedience to his parents and in their service. People would have had blessing and joy by seeing this. However, God's commandment was not permitted to be commended with such care and diligence. It had to be neglected and trampled under foot [Matthew 7:6], so that a child could not take it to heart. Meanwhile, the child would gape like a panting wolf at the things we set up, without once ‹consulting or› giving reverence to God. 114

For God's sake, let us learn this at last: placing all other things out of sight, let our youths look first to this commandment if they wish to serve God with truly good works. Then they may do what is pleasing to their fathers and mothers, or to those to whom they may be subject instead of parents. For every child that knows and does this 115

has, in the first place, this great consolation in his heart. He can joyfully say and boast (in spite of and against all who are occupied with works of their own choice): "Behold, this work is well pleasing to my God in heaven, that I know for
116 certain." Let them all come together with their many great, distressing, and difficult works and make their boast. We will see whether they can show one work that is greater and nobler than obedience to father and mother. For to parents God has appointed and commanded obedience next to His own majesty. For if God's Word and will are in force and being accomplished, nothing shall be valued higher than the will and word of parents, as long as that, too, is subordinated to obedience toward God and is not opposed to the preceding commandments.

117 Therefore, you should be heartily glad and thank God that He has chosen you and made you worthy to do a work so precious and pleasing to Him. Only note this: although this work is regarded as the most humble and despised, consider it great and precious. Do this not because of the worthiness of parents, but because this work is included in, and controlled by, the jewel and sanctuary, namely, the Word and commandment
118 of God. Oh, what a high price all Carthusians,

monks, and nuns would pay if in all their religious activities they could bring into God's presence a single work done by virtue of His commandment, and if they were able to say with joyful heart before His face, "Now I know that this work is well pleasing to You!" Where will these poor wretched persons hide when, in the sight of God and all the world, they shall blush with shame before a young child who has lived according to this commandment [Matthew 18:1–4]? Will they not have to confess that with their whole life that they are not worthy to give that child a drink of water [Mark
9:41]? It serves them right. Because of their devil- 119
ish perversion in treading God's commandment under foot, they must vainly torment themselves with works of their own making and, in addition, have scorn and loss for their reward.

Should not the heart, then, leap and melt for 120
joy when going to work and doing what is commanded, saying: Look! This is better than all the holiness of the Carthusians, even though they kill themselves fasting and praying upon their knees without ceasing! For here you have a sure text and a divine testimony that God has commanded this. But concerning the holiness of Carthusians He did not command a word. This is the plight and miserable blindness of the world [2 Corinthians

4:4]. No one believes these things. The devil has deceived us to such an extent with false holiness and the glamour of our own works.

121 I would be very glad—I say it again—if people would open their eyes and ears and take this to heart, lest someday we should again be led astray from God's pure Word [Psalm 12:6] to the devil's lying vanities [Psalm 31:6]. If people would take this to heart, all would be well. For parents would have more joy, love, friendship, and unity in their houses. The children could captivate their par-
122 ents' hearts. On the other hand, when children are stubborn and will not do what they ought until a rod is laid upon their back [Proverbs 22:15; 26:3], they anger both God and their parents. In this way they deprive themselves of this treasure and joy of conscience, and they lay up for them-
123 selves only misfortune. As everyone complains, the course of the world now is such that both young and old completely lack restraint and are beyond control. They have no reverence or sense of honor. They do nothing unless they are driven to it by blows, and they do what wrong and slander they can behind each other's back. Therefore, God also punishes them, so that they sink into all
124 kinds of filth and misery. As a rule, the parents, too, are themselves stupid and ignorant. One fool

trains another. As the foolish parents have lived, so live their children after them.

This, now, I say should be the first and most 125
important consideration that urges us to keep
this commandment. Because of this, even if we
had no father and mother, we should wish that
God would set up wood and stone before us, so
that we might call them father and mother. Since
He has given us living parents, how much more
should we rejoice to show them honor and obedience? For we know it is so highly pleasing to the
Divine Majesty and to all angels, and it harasses
all devils. Besides, this is the highest work we can
do, after the grand divine worship included in
the previous commandments. Giving to the poor 126
and every other good work toward our neighbor
is not equal to this. For God has assigned parenthood the highest place. Yes, He has set it up in
His own place upon the earth. God's will and
pleasure ought to be enough reason and incen-
tive for us to do what we can with good will and
pleasure.

Besides this, it is our duty before the world 127
to be grateful for benefits and every good that
we have from our parents. But here again the 128
devil rules in the world [Ephesians 6:12], so that
the children forget their parents. We all forget

God, and no one considers how God nourishes, protects, and defends us, and how He bestows so much good on body and soul [Psalm 23]. This is especially true when an evil time comes. We grow angry and grumble with impatience, and all the good that we have received throughout our life is wiped out ‹of our memory [Psalm 78:17–31]›. We act the same way toward our parents, and there is no child that understands and considers ‹what the parents have endured while nourishing and fostering him›, unless the Holy Spirit grants him this grace.

129 God knows very well this perverseness of the world; therefore, He admonishes and urges by commandments that everyone consider what his parents have done for him. Each child will discover that he has from them a body and life. He has been fed and reared when otherwise he would have perished a hundred times in his own
130 filth. Therefore, this is a true and good saying of old and wise people: "To God, to parents, and to teachers we can never offer enough thanks and compensation." The person who thinks about and considers this will give all honor to his parents without force and bear them up on his hands as those through whom God has done him all good [Psalm 91:12].

Over and above all this, another great reason that should move us more to obey this commandment is that God attaches to it a temporal promise: "That your days may be long in the land that the Lord your God is giving you" [Exodus 20:12]. 131

From this you can see for yourself how serious God is about this commandment. He not only declares that it is well pleasing to Him and that He has joy and delight in it, but He also declares that it shall prosper us and promote our highest good, so that we may have a pleasant and agreeable life, 132
furnished with every good thing. Therefore, St. 133
Paul also greatly emphasizes the same promise and rejoices in it when he says that this is the first commandment with a promise, "that it may go well with you and that you may live long in the land" (Ephesians 6:2–3). Although the rest of the commandments have promises in them, none is so plainly and clearly stated.

Here, then, you have learned the fruit and the reward, that whoever keeps this commandment shall have happy days, fortune, and prosperity. On the other hand, you also have learned the punishment, that whoever is disobedient shall perish sooner and never enjoy life. For to have long life in the sense of the Scriptures is not only to become old, but to have everything that 134

belongs to long life: health, wife, children, livelihood, peace, good government, and so on. Without these things this life can neither be enjoyed in
135 cheerfulness nor long endure. If, therefore, you will not obey father and mother and submit to their discipline, then obey the hangman. If you will not obey him, then submit to the skeleton
136 man (i.e., death). For God will insist on this in sum: if you obey Him, offering love and service, He will reward you abundantly with all good. If you offend Him, He will send upon you both death and the hangman.

137 Where do so many rogues come from that must daily be hanged, beheaded, and broken upon the wheel? Don't they come from disobedience to parents, because they will not submit to discipline in kindness? By God's punishment, they cause us to behold their misfortune and grief. For it seldom happens that such perverse people die a natural or timely death.

But the godly and obedient have this blessing: they live long in pleasant quietness and see their children's children (as said above) to the third and fourth generation [Psalm 128].

138 Experience teaches that where there are honorable, old families who do well and have many children, they certainly owe their origin to the

fact that some of them were brought up well and were full of regard for their parents. On the other hand, it is written of the wicked, "May his posterity be cut off; may his name be blotted out in the
second generation!" (Psalm 109:13). Therefore, 139
note well how great a thing in God's sight obedience is. He values it so highly, is so highly pleased with it, and rewards it richly. He also enforces punishment rigorously on those who act against it.

All this I say that it may be well impressed 140
upon the young [Deuteronomy 6:7]. No one believes how necessary this commandment is, although it has not been valued and taught under the papacy up to this point. These are simple and easy words, and everybody thought he knew them before. Therefore, people pass by them lightly, crave other things, and do not see and believe that God is so greatly offended if these words are disregarded. They don't see that a person does a work so well pleasing and precious if he follows them.

In this commandment belongs a further state- 141
ment about all kinds of obedience to persons in authority who have to command and to govern. For all authority flows and is born from the authority of parents. Where a father is unable alone

to educate his ‹rebellious and irritable› child, he uses a schoolmaster to teach the child. If he is too weak, he gets the help of his friends and neighbors. If he departs this life, he delegates and confers his authority and government upon oth-
142 ers who are appointed for the purpose. Likewise, a father must have domestic manservants and maidservants under himself for the management of the household. So all whom we call "masters" are in the place of parents and must get their power and authority to govern from them. So also men are all called fathers in the Scriptures, who in their government perform the functions of a father, and have a paternal heart toward their subordinates. From antiquity the Romans and other nations called the masters and mistresses of the household "housefathers" and "housemothers." They called their national rulers and overlords "fathers of the entire country." This is a great shame to us who would be Christians because we do not give them the same title or, at least, do not value and honor them as fathers.

143 Now, the honor a child owes to a father and mother is owed by all who are included in the household. Therefore, manservants and maidservants should be careful to be obedient to their masters and mistresses. They should also honor

them as their own fathers and mothers and do everything they know is expected of them, not forced and unwillingly, but with pleasure and joy because of what I just mentioned—it is God's command and is pleasing to Him above all other
works. They ought to pay for the privilege and 144
be glad they may get masters and mistresses so that they may have such joyful consciences and know how they may do truly golden works. This is a matter that has been neglected and despised till now. Instead, everybody ran—in the devil's name—into convents or to pilgrimages and indulgences, with loss of time and money and with an evil conscience.

If this truth, then, could be impressed upon 145
the poor people, a servant girl would leap and praise and thank God. With her tidy work, for which she receives support and wages, she would gain such a treasure of good works. It would be unlike all those gained by people regarded by saints. Is it not an excellent boast to know and say that if you perform your daily domestic task, this is better than all the sanctity and ascetic life of
monks? You have the promise, in addition, that 146
you shall prosper in all good and fare well. How can you lead a more blessed or holier life as far as
your works are concerned? In God's sight faith 147

is what really makes a person holy and serves Him alone [Romans 4:3–5], but the works are for
148 the service of people. There you have everything good: protection and defense in the Lord, a joyful conscience, and a gracious God besides. He will reward you a hundredfold [Matthew 19:27–29], so that you are like a knight if you are only pious and obedient. But if you are not, you have, in the first place, nothing but God's wrath and displeasure, no peace of heart, and afterward, all kinds of plagues and misfortunes.

149 Whoever will not be moved by this and lean toward godliness we hand over to the hangman and to the skeleton man. Therefore, let everyone who allows himself to be advised remember that God is not joking. Know that it is God who speaks with you and demands obedience. If you obey Him, you are His dear child [John 14:23]. But if you despise obedience, then take shame, misery, and grief for your reward.

150 The same should also be said about obedience to civil government. This (as we have said) is all included in the place of fatherhood and extends farthest of all relations. Here "father" is not one person from a single family, but it means the many people the father has as tenants, citizens, or subjects. Through them, as through our parents,

God gives to us food, house and home, protection, and security. They bear such name and title with all honor as their highest dignity that it is our duty to honor them and to value them greatly as the dearest treasure and the most precious jewel upon earth.

The person who is obedient in this is willing 151
and ready to serve. He cheerfully does all that deals with honor. He knows that he is pleasing God and that he will receive joy and happiness for his reward. If he will not do this in love, but despises and resists authority or rebels, let him also know that he shall have no favor or blessing. Where he thinks he will gain a florin, he will lose ten times as much elsewhere. Or he will become a victim to the hangman, perish by war, pestilence, or famine. He will experience no good in his children and be obliged to suffer injury, injustice, and violence at the hands of his servants, neighbors, or strangers and tyrants. For what we seek and deserve is paid back and comes home to us [Galatians 6:7].

If we would ever allow ourselves to be per- 152
suaded that such works are pleasing to God and have so rich a reward, we would be completely established in abundant possessions and have what our heart desires [Psalm 37:4]. But because God's

Word and command are so lightly esteemed, as
though some peddler had spoken it, let us see
whether you are the person to oppose Him. How
difficult, do you think, it will be for God to pay
153 you back! You would certainly live much better
with divine favor, peace, and happiness than with
154 His displeasure and misfortune. Why do you
think the world is now so full of unfaithfulness,
disgrace, calamity, and murder? It is because
everyone desires to be his own master and free
from the emperor, to care nothing for anyone,
and to do what pleases him. Therefore, God punishes one knave by another, so that, when you
defraud and despise your master, another comes
and deals in the same way with you. Yes, in your
household you must suffer ten times more from
wife, children, or servants.

155 We feel our misfortune, we murmur and
complain of unfaithfulness, violence, and injustice. But we refuse to see that we ourselves are
knaves who have fully deserved this punishment.
And even by this we are not reformed. We will
have no favor and happiness. Therefore, it is only
fair that we have nothing but misfortune with-
156 out mercy. There must still be somewhere upon
earth some godly people, because God continues
to grant us so much good! On our own account,

we should not have a farthing in the house nor a
straw in the field. All this I have been obliged to 157
urge with so many words, in the hope that someone may take it to heart. Then we may be relieved of the blindness and misery in which we are stuck so deeply. Then we may truly understand God's Word and will, and seriously accept it. We would learn how we could have joy, happiness, and salvation enough, both now and eternally.

So we have two kinds of fathers presented in 158
this commandment: fathers in blood and fathers in office. Or, those who have the care of the family and those who have the care of the country. Besides these there are still spiritual fathers. They are not like those in the papacy, who have had themselves called fathers but have performed no function of the fatherly office [Matthew 23:9]. For the only ones called spiritual fathers are those who govern and guide us by God's Word.
In this sense, St. Paul boasts his fatherhood in 159
1 Corinthians 4:15, where he says, "I became your father in Christ Jesus through the gospel."
Now, since they are fathers, they are entitled to 160
their honor, even above all others. But to spiritual fathers the least amount of honor is bestowed. The way the world knows for honoring them is to drive them out of the country and to begrudge

them a piece of bread. In short, spiritual fathers must be (as says St. Paul [1 Corinthians 4:13]) like the filth of the world and everybody's refuse and footrag.

161 Yet there is need that this truth about spiritual
fatherhood also be taught to the people. For those
who want to be Christians are obliged in God's
sight to think them worthy of double honor who
minister to their souls [1 Timothy 5:17–18]. They
are obligated to deal well with them and provide
for them. For that reason, God is willing to bless
162 you enough and will not let you run out. But
in this matter everyone refuses to be generous
and resists. All are afraid that they will perish
from bodily needs and cannot now support one
respectable preacher, where formerly they filled
163 ten potbellies. Because of this, we also deserve for
God to deprive us of His Word and blessing and
to allow preachers of lies to arise again and lead
us to the devil. In addition, they will drain our
sweat and blood.

164 But those who keep God's will and commandment in sight have this promise: everything they give to temporal and spiritual fathers, and whatever they do to honor them, shall be richly repaid to them. They will not have bread, clothing, and money for a year or two, but will have long life,

support, and peace. They shall be eternally rich and blessed. So just do what is your duty. Let God 165
manage how He will support you and provide enough for you. Since He has promised it and has never lied yet, He will not be found lying to you [Titus 1:2].

This ought to encourage us and give us hearts 166
that would melt in pleasure and love for those to whom we owe honor. We ought to raise our hands [1 Timothy 2:8] and joyfully thank God, who has given us such promises. For such promises we ought to run to the ends of the world‹, to the remotest parts of India›. For although the whole world should work together, it could not add an hour to our life [Matthew 6:27] or give us a single grain from the earth. But God wishes to give you everything exceedingly and abundantly according to your heart's desire [Psalm 37:4]. He who despises and casts this promise to the winds is not worthy ever to hear a word about God. More than enough has now been stated for all who belong under this commandment.

In addition, it would be well to preach to the 167
parents also, and to those who bear their office. Tell them how they should behave toward those who are given to them for their governance. This is not stated in the Ten Commandments. But it

is still abundantly commanded in many places in the Scripture. God wants to have this included in this commandment when He speaks of father
168 and mother. He does not wish to have rogues and tyrants in this office and government. He does not assign this honor to them, that is, power and authority to govern, so they can have themselves worshiped. But they should consider that they are obligated to obey God. First of all, they should seriously and faithfully fulfill their office, not only to support and provide for the bodily necessities of their children, servants, subjects, and so on, but, most of all, they should train them to honor
169 and praise God [Proverbs 22:6]. Therefore, do not think that this matter is left to your pleasure and arbitrary will. This is God's strict command and order, to whom also you must give account for it [1 Peter 4:5].

170 Here again the sad plight arises that no one sees or hears this truth. All live on as though God gave us children for our pleasure or amusement and servants so that we could use them like a cow or an ass, only for work. Or they live as though we were only to gratify our lewd behavior with our subjects, ignoring them, as though we have no
171 concern for what they learn or how they live. No one is willing to see that this is the command of

the Supreme Majesty, who will most strictly call
us to account and punish us for it. Nor does anyone see that there is so much need to be seriously
concerned about the young. For if we wish to 172
have excellent and able persons both for civil and
Church leadership, we must spare no diligence,
time, or cost in teaching and educating our children, so that they may serve God and the world.
We must not think only about how we may amass 173
money and possessions for them. God can indeed
support and make them rich without us, as He
daily does. But for this purpose He has given us
children and issued this command: we should
train and govern them according to His will.
Otherwise, He would have no purpose for a father
and a mother. Therefore, let everyone know that 174
it is his duty, on peril of losing the divine favor, to
bring up his children in the fear and knowledge
of God above all things [Proverbs 1:7]. And if the
children are talented, have them learn and study
something. Then they may be hired for whatever
need there is.

If that were done, God would also richly bless 175
us and give us grace to train men by whom land
and people might be improved. He would also
bless us with well-educated citizens, chaste and
domestic wives, who, afterward, would raise

176 godly children and servants. Here consider now
what deadly harm you are doing if you are negligent and fail on your part to bring up your children to usefulness and piety. Consider how you bring upon yourself all sin and wrath, earning hell by your own children, even though you are
177 otherwise pious and holy. Because this matter is disregarded, God so fearfully punishes the world that there is no discipline, government, or peace. We all complain about this but do not see that it is our fault. The way we train children and subjects spoils them and makes them disobedient.
178 Let this be enough encouragement. To draw this out further belongs to another time.

THE FIFTH COMMANDMENT

179 **You shall not murder.**

180 We have now finished teaching about both the spiritual and the temporal government, that is, the divine and the parental authority and obedience. But now we go forth from our house among our neighbors to learn how we should live with one another, everyone himself toward
181 his neighbor. Therefore, God and government are not included in this commandment. Nor is the power to kill taken away, which God and

government have. To punish evildoers, God has delegated His authority to the government, not parents. In earlier times, as we read in Moses, parents were required to bring their own children to judgment and even to sentence them to death [Deuteronomy 21:18–21]. Therefore, what is forbidden in this commandment is forbidden to the individual in his relationship with anyone else, but not to the government.

Now, this commandment is easy enough 182
and has often been presented, because we hear it each year in the Gospel of St. Matthew 5:20–26, where Christ Himself explains and sums it up. He says that we must not kill, neither with hand, heart, mouth, signs, gestures, help, nor counsel. Therefore, this commandment forbids everyone to be angry, except those (as we said) who are in the place of God, that is, parents and the government. For it is proper for God and for everyone who is in a divine estate to be angry, to rebuke, and to punish because of those very persons who transgress this and the other commandments [Romans 13:4].

The cause and need of this commandment is 183
that God well knows that the world is evil [Galatians 1:4], and that this life has much unhappiness. Therefore, He has set up this and the other

commandments between the good people and the evil. Now, just as there are many attacks on all commandments, so the same happens also with this commandment. We must live among many people who do us harm, and we have a reason to be hostile to them.

184 For example, when your neighbor sees that you have a better house and home, ‹a larger family and more fertile fields,› greater possessions and fortune from God than he does, he gets in a bad mood, envies you, and speaks no good of you.

So by the devil's encouragement you will get many enemies who cannot bear to see you have any good, either bodily or spiritual. When we see such people, our hearts also would like to rage and bleed and take vengeance. Then there arise cursing and blows. From them misery and
185 murder finally come. In this commandment God—like a kind father—steps in ahead of us, intervenes, and wishes to have the quarrel settled, so that no misfortune comes from it and no one destroys another person. And briefly, He would in this way protect, set free, and keep in peace everyone against the crime and violence of everyone else. He would have this commandment placed as a wall, fortress, and refuge around our neighbor so that we do not hurt or harm him in his body.

The commandment has this goal, that no one 186
would offend his neighbor because of any evil deed, even though he has fully deserved it. For where murder is forbidden, all cause from which murder may spring is also forbidden. For many people, although they do not kill, curse and utter a wish that would stop a person from running
far if it were to strike him on the neck. Now, this 187
urge dwells in everyone by nature. It is common practice that no one is willing to suffer at the hands of another person. Therefore, God wants to remove the root and source by which the heart is embittered against our neighbor. He wants to make us used to keeping this commandment ever in view, always to contemplate ourselves in it as in a mirror [James 1:23–25], to regard the will of God, and to turn over to Him the wrong that we suffer with hearty confidence and by calling on His name. In this way we shall let our enemies rage and be angry, doing what they can. We learn to calm our wrath and to have a patient, gentle heart, especially toward those who give us cause to be angry (i.e., our enemies).

Therefore, the entire sum of what it means *not* 188
to murder is to be impressed most clearly upon the simpleminded [Deuteronomy 6:7]. In the first place, we must harm no one, either with our

hand or by deed. We must not use our tongue to instigate or counsel harm. We must neither use nor agree to use any means or methods by which another person may be injured. Finally, the heart must not be ill disposed toward anyone or wish another person ill in anger and hatred. Then body and soul may be innocent toward everyone, but especially toward those who wish you evil or inflict such things upon you. For to do evil to someone who wishes you good and does you good is not human, but devilish.

189 Second, a person who does evil to his neighbor is not the only one guilty under this commandment. It also applies to anyone who can do his neighbor good, prevent or resist evil, defend, and save his neighbor so that no bodily harm or hurt happen to him—yet does not do this [James
190 2:15–16]. If, therefore, you send away someone who is naked when you could clothe him, you have caused him to freeze to death. If you see someone suffer hunger and do not give him food, you have caused him to starve. So also, if you see anyone innocently sentenced to death or in similar distress, and do not save him, although you know ways and means to do so, you have killed him. It will not work for you to make the excuse that you did not provide any help, counsel,

or aid to harm him. For you have withheld your love from him and deprived him of the benefit by which his life would have been saved.

God also rightly calls all people murderers 191
who do not provide counsel and help in distress and danger of body and life. He will pass a most terrible sentence upon them in the Last Day, as Christ Himself has announced that He will say, "I was hungry and you gave Me no food, I was thirsty and you gave Me no drink, I was a stranger and you did not welcome Me, naked and you did not clothe Me, sick and in prison and you did not visit Me" [Matthew 25:42–43]. This means: You would have allowed Me and Mine to die of hunger, thirst, and cold. You would have allowed the wild beasts to tear us to pieces, or left us to rot in
prison or perish in distress. What else is that but 192
to rebuke them as murderers and bloodhounds? For although you have not actually done all this to someone, you have still, so far as you were concerned, let him wither and perish in misfortune.

It is just as if I saw someone navigating and laboring in deep water, or one fallen into fire, and could extend to him the hand to pull him out and save him, and yet refused to do it. How would I look, even in the eyes of the world? Just like a murderer and a criminal.

193 Therefore, it is God's ultimate purpose that we
let harm come to no one, but show him all good
194 and love. As we have said, this commandment is
especially directed toward those who are our enemies. For to do good to our friends is an ordinary
heathen virtue, as Christ says in Matthew 5:46.

195 Here again we have God's Word, by which He would encourage and teach us to do true, noble, and grand works such as gentleness, patience, and, in short, love and kindness to our enemies [Galatians 5:22–23]. He would ever remind us to reflect upon the First Commandment—He is our God, which means He will help, assist, and protect us in order that He may quench the desire of revenge in us.

196 We ought to practice and teach this; then we
would have our hands full by doing good works.
197 But this would not be preaching for monks. It
would greatly undermine from the religious calling and interfere with the sanctity of Carthusians.
It would even be regarded as forbidding good
works and clearing the convents. For the ordinary
state of Christians would be considered just as
worthy—and even worthier than monastic life.
Everybody would see how the Carthusians mock
and delude the world with a false, hypocritical

show of holiness [Matthew 23:27], because they have cast this and other commandments to the winds. They have considered them unnecessary, as though they were not commandments, but mere "evangelical counsels." At the same time, they have shamelessly proclaimed and boasted about their hypocritical calling and works as the most perfect life. They do this so that they might lead a pleasant, easy life, without the cross and without patience. For this reason also, they have created the cloisters, so that they might not be obliged to suffer any wrong from anyone or to
do that person any good. But know now that the 198
works of this commandment are the true, holy, and godly works. God rejoices in them with all the angels. In comparison with these works all human holiness is just stench and filth [Isaiah 64:6]. And besides, human holiness deserves nothing but wrath and damnation.

THE SIXTH COMMANDMENT

You shall not commit adultery. 199

The following commandments are easily un- 200
derstood from the explanation of the preceding commandments. For they are all to show that we must avoid doing any kind of harm to our

neighbor. But they are arranged in fine order. In the first place, they talk about our neighbor personally. Then they proceed to talk about the person nearest him, or the closest possession next after his body, namely, his wife. She is one flesh and blood with him [Genesis 2:23–24], so that we cannot inflict a higher injury upon him in any good that is his. Therefore, it is clearly forbidden here to bring any disgrace upon our neighbor re-
201 garding his wife. The commandment really takes aim at adultery, because among the Jewish people it was ordained and commanded that everyone must be married. The young were engaged to be married early, and the virgin state was held in small esteem. Yet neither were public prostitution and lewdness tolerated (as now). Therefore, adultery was the most common form of unchastity among them.

202 But among us there is such a shameful mess and the very dregs of all vice and lewdness. Therefore, this commandment is directed against all kinds of unchastity, whatever it may be called.
203 Not only is the outward act of adultery forbidden, but also every kind of cause, motive, and means of adultery. Then the heart, the lips, and the whole body may be chaste and offer no opportunity,
204 help, or persuasion toward inchastity. Not only

this, but we must also resist temptation, offer protection, and rescue honor wherever there is danger and need. We must give help and counsel, so as to maintain our neighbor's honor. For whenever you abandon this effort when you could resist unchastity, or whenever you overlook it as if it did not concern you, you are as truly guilty of adultery
as the one doing the deed. To speak in the briefest 205
way, this much is required of you: everyone must live chastely himself and help his neighbor do the same. So by this commandment God wishes to build a hedge round about [Job 1:10] and protect every spouse so that no one trespasses against him or her.

But this commandment is aimed directly at 206
the state of marriage and gives us an opportunity to speak about it. First, understand and mark well how gloriously God honors and praises this estate. For by His commandment He both approves and guards it. He has approved it above in the Fourth Commandment, "Honor your father and your mother." But here He has (as we said)
hedged it about and protected it. Therefore, He 207
also wishes us to honor it [Hebrews 13:4] and to maintain and govern it as a divine and blessed estate because, in the first place, He has instituted it before all others. He created man and woman

separately, as is clear [Genesis 1:27]. This was not for lewdness, but so that they might live together in marriage, be fruitful, bear children, and nourish and train them to honor God [Genesis 1:28; Psalm 128; Proverbs 22:6; Ephesians 6:4].

208 Therefore, God has also most richly blessed this estate above all others. In addition, He has bestowed on it and wrapped up in it everything in the world, so that this estate might be well and richly provided for. Married life is, therefore, no joke or presumption. It is an excellent thing and a matter of divine seriousness. For marriage has the highest importance to God so that people are raised up who may serve the world and promote the knowledge of God, godly living, and all virtues, to fight against wickedness and the devil.

209 I have always taught that this estate should not be despised nor held in disrepute, as is done by the blind world and our false Church leaders. Marriage should be regarded as it is in God's Word, where it is adorned and sanctified. It is not only placed on an equality with other estates, but it comes first and surpasses them all—emperor, princes, bishops, or whoever they please. For both Church and civil estates must humble themselves and all be found in this estate, as we shall
210 hear. Therefore, it is not a peculiar estate, but

the most common and noblest estate that runs through all Christendom. Yes, it extends through all the world.

In the second place, you must know also that marriage is not only an honorable but also a necessary state. In general and in all conditions it is solemnly commanded by God that men and women, who were created for marriage, shall be found in this estate. Yet there are some exceptions (although few) whom God has especially set apart. They are not fit for the married estate. Or there are individuals whom He has released by a high, supernatural gift so that they can maintain chastity without this estate [Matthew 19:11–12]. 211
For where nature has its course—since it is given by God—it is not possible to remain chaste without marriage [1 Corinthians 7]. For flesh and blood remain flesh and blood. The natural desire and excitement have their course without delay or hindrance, as everybody sees and feels. In order, therefore, that it may be easier in some degree to avoid inchastity, God has commanded the estate of marriage. In this way everyone may have his proper portion and be satisfied with it. Yet God's grace is also required in order that the heart may be pure. 212

From this you see how this popish rabble 213

—priests, monks, and nuns—resist God's order and commandment. For they despise and forbid matrimony, and they dare and vow to maintain perpetual chastity. Besides this, they deceive the simpleminded with lying words and appearances.
214 For no one has so little love and desire for chastity as these very people. Because of great sanctity, they avoid marriage and either indulge in open and shameless prostitution or secretly do even
215 worse, so that one dare not speak of it. Unfortunately this has been learned too fully. In short, even though they abstain from the act, their hearts are so full of unchaste thoughts and evil lusts that there is a continual burning and secret suffering, which can be avoided in the married life [1 Corin-
216 thians 7:9]. Therefore, all vows of chastity outside of the married state are condemned by this commandment. Free permission to marry is granted. Indeed, even the command is given to all poor ensnared consciences that have been deceived by their monastic vows: abandon the unchaste state and enter the married life. They must consider that even if the monastic life were godly, it would still not be in their power to maintain chastity. And if they remain in their monastic vows, they must only sin more and more against this commandment.

Now, I speak of this in order that the young 217
may be guided so that they desire the married
estate and know that it is a blessed estate and
pleases God. For in this way, over time we might
cause married life to be restored to honor. There
might be less of the filthy, loose, disorderly behavior that now run riot the world over in open
prostitution and other shameful vices arising
from disregard for married life. Therefore, it is 218
the duty of parents and the government to see to
it that our youth are brought up with discipline
and respectability. When they have become mature, parents and government should provide for
them to marry in the fear of God and honorably.
God would not fail to add His blessing and grace,
so that people would have joy and happiness
from marriage.

Let me now say in conclusion what this com- 219
mandment demands: Everyone should live chaste
in thought, word, and deed in his condition—that
is, especially in the estate of marriage. But also
everyone should love and value the spouse God
gave to him [Ephesians 5:33]. For where marital
chastity is to be maintained, man and wife must
by all means live together in love and harmony.
Then one may cherish the other from the heart
and with complete faithfulness. For harmony is

one of the principal points that enkindles love
and desire for chastity, so that, where this is
found, chastity will follow without any command.
220 Therefore, St. Paul diligently encourages husband
221 and wife to love and honor one another. Here
you have again precious, indeed, many and great
good works. You can joyfully boast about them,
against all churchly estates chosen without God's
Word and commandment.

THE SEVENTH COMMANDMENT

222 **You shall not steal.**

223 After the commandment about you personally and your spouse, next comes the commandment about temporal property. God also wants
property protected. He has commanded that no
one shall take away from, or diminish, his neigh-
224 bor's possessions. For to steal is nothing else than
to get possession of another's property wrongfully. Briefly, this includes all kinds of advantage
in all sorts of trade to the disadvantage of our
neighbor. Now, this is indeed quite a widespread
and common vice. But it is so little considered
and noticed that it surpasses all measure. So if all
thieves who did not want to be known as thieves
were to be hanged on gallows, the world would

soon be devastated. There would be a lack both of executioners and gallows. For, as we have just said, to "steal" means not only emptying our neighbor's money box and pockets. It also means grasping property in the market, in all stores, booths, wine and beer cellars, workshops, and, in short, wherever there is trading or taking and giving of money for merchandise or labor.

Let me explain this somewhat plainly for the 225
common people, that it may be seen how godly we are. For example, consider a manservant or maidservant who does not serve faithfully in the house, does damage, or allows damage to be done when it could be prevented. He ruins and neglects the goods entrusted to him, by laziness, idleness, or hate, to the spite and sorrow of master and mistress. In whatever way this can be done purposely (I'm not talking about what happens by mistake and against one's will), you can in a year steal thirty or forty florins. If another servant had taken that much money secretly or carried it away, he would be hanged with the rope. But here you (while conscious of such a great theft) may even express defiance and become rude, and no one dare call you a thief.

I say the same also about mechanics, work- 226
men, and day laborers. They all follow their

evil thoughts and never know enough ways to overcharge people, while they are lazy and unfaithful in their work. All these are far worse than burglars, whom we can guard against with locks and bolts and, if caught, can be treated in such a way that they will not commit the crime again. But against unfaithful workers no one can guard. No one even dares to give them an angry look or accuse them of theft. One would rather lose ten times as much money from his purse. For here are my neighbors, good friends, my own servants, from whom I expect ‹every faithful and diligent service›, yet they cheat me most of all.

227 Furthermore, in the market and in common trade also, this practice is in full swing and force to the greatest extent. There one openly cheats another with bad merchandise; false measures, weights, and coins; and by nimbleness and strange finances [Proverbs 20:10]. Or he takes advantage of him with clever tricks. Likewise, one overcharges another in a trade and greedily drives a hard bargain, skins and distresses him.
228 Who can repeat or think of all these acts? To sum up, this is the most common trade and the largest union on earth. If we consider the world through all conditions of life, it is nothing but a vast, wide sales booth, full of great thieves.

Therefore, some are also called swivel-chair robbers, land and highway robbers, not picklocks and burglars. For they snatch away easy money, but they sit on a chair at home and are styled great noblemen and honorable, pious citizens. They rob and steal in a way assumed to be good. 229

Yes, here we might be silent about the petty individual thieves if we were to attack the great, powerful archthieves with whom lords and princes keep company. These thieves daily plunder not only a city or two, but all of Germany. Indeed, where should we place the head and supreme protector of all thieves—the Holy Chair at Rome with all its train of attendants—which has grabbed by theft the wealth of all the world, and holds it to this day? 230

This is, in short, the way of the world: whoever can steal and rob openly goes free and secure, unmolested by anyone, and even demands that he be honored. Meanwhile, the little burglars, who have once trespassed, must bear the shame and punishment to make the former thieves appear godly and honorable. But let such open thieves know that in God's sight they are the greatest thieves. He will punish them as they are worthy and deserve. 231

Now, since this commandment is so 232

far-reaching, as just indicated, it is necessary to teach it well and to explain it to the common people. Do not let them go on in their greed and security. But always place before their eyes God's wrath, and instill the same. For we must preach this not to Christians, but chiefly to hoods and scoundrels. It would be more fitting for judges, jailers, or Master Hans (the executioner) to
233 preach to them. Therefore, let everyone know his duty, at the risk of God's displeasure: he must do no harm to his neighbor nor deprive him of profit nor commit any act of unfaithfulness or hatred in any bargain or trade. But he must also faithfully preserve his property for him, secure and promote his advantage. This is especially true when one accepts money, wages, and one's livelihood for such service.

234 Now the person who greedily despises this commandment may indeed pass by and escape the hangman. But he shall not escape God's wrath and punishment [Galatians 6:7–8; 1 Thessalonians 5:3]. When he has long practiced his defiance and arrogance, he shall still remain a tramp and beggar. In addition, he will have all
235 plagues and misfortune. Now you are going your own way, though you ought to preserve the property of your master and mistress. For your

service you fill your throat and stomach, take your wages like a thief, and have people treat you like a nobleman. For there are many that are even rude towards their masters and mistresses and are unwilling to do them a favor or service by which to protect them from loss.

But consider what you will gain. When you 236
have come into your own property and are set up in your home (to which God will help with all misfortunes), your earlier misdeeds will bob up again and come home to you. You will find that where you have cheated or done injury at the value of one mite, you will have to pay thirty again.

This will also be the result for craftsmen and 237
day laborers. We are now obliged to hear and suffer such intolerable hatred from them, as though they were noblemen in another's possessions and everyone is obliged to give them what they
demand. Just let them continue making their de- 238
mands as long as they can. God will not forget His commandment. He will reward them just as they have served. He will hang them, not upon a green gallows, but upon a dry one. So all their life they
shall neither prosper nor gather anything. In- 239
deed, if there were a well-ordered government in the land, such greediness might soon be checked

and prevented. That was the custom in ancient times among the Romans. There such characters were promptly seized by the head in a way that caused others to take warning.

240 No more shall all the rest prosper who change the open, free market into a flesh pit of extortion and a den of robbery [Luke 19:46], where the poor are daily overcharged, and where new burdens and high prices are imposed. Everyone there uses the market according to his whim. He is even defiant and brags as though it were his fair privilege and right to sell his goods for as high a price as he pleases, and no one had a right to say
241 a word against it. We will indeed look on and let
242 these people skin, pinch, and hoard. But we will trust in God, who will do the following: after you have been skinning and scraping for a long time, He will pronounce such a blessing on your gains that your grain in the silo, your beer in the cellar, and your cattle in the stalls shall perish [Luke 12:16–21]. Yes, where you have cheated and overcharged anyone for even a florin, your entire pile of wealth shall be consumed with rust, so that you shall never enjoy it [Matthew 6:19; James 5:1–3].

243 Indeed, we see and experience this being fulfilled daily before our eyes. No stolen or dishonestly acquired possession thrives. How many

there are who rake and scrape day and night,
and yet grow not a farthing richer! Though they
gather much, they must suffer so many plagues
and misfortunes that they cannot enjoy it with
cheerfulness nor leave it to their children. But 244
since no one cares, and we go on as though it
did not concern us, God must visit us in a different way and teach us manners by imposing one taxation after another. Or He must billet a troop of soldiers upon us. In one hour they empty our moneyboxes and purses and do not quit as long as we have a farthing left. In addition, by way of thanks, they burn and devastate house and home, and they outrage and kill wife and children.

In short, if you steal much, you can expect 245
that much will be stolen from you. He who robs and gets by violence and wrong will submit to one who shall act the same way toward him. For God is master of this art. Since everyone robs and steals from one another, God punishes one thief by means of another. Or else where would we find enough gallows and ropes?

Now, whoever is willing to be instructed, let 246
him know that this is God's commandment. It must not be treated as a joke. For although you despise, defraud, steal, and rob us, we will indeed manage to endure your arrogance, suffer,

and—according to the Lord's Prayer—forgive and show pity [Matthew 6:12]. For we know that the godly shall nevertheless have enough [Psalm 37:25]. But you injure yourself more than another.

247 Beware of this: The poor man will come to you (there are so many now). He must buy things with the penny of his daily wages and live upon it. When you are harsh to him, as though everyone lived by your favor, and you skin and scrape him to the bone, and when you turn him away with pride and arrogance to whom you ought to give things without payment, he will go away wretched and sorrowful. Since he can complain to no one else, he will cry and call to heaven [Psalm 20:6; 146:8–9]. Then beware (I say again) as of the devil himself. For such groaning and calling will be no joke. It will have a weight that will prove too heavy for you and all the world. For it will reach Him who takes care of the poor, sorrowful hearts. He will not allow them to go unavenged [Isaiah 61:1–3]. But if you despise this and become defiant, see the One you have brought upon you. If you succeed and prosper, before all the world you may call God and me a liar.

248 We have exhorted, warned, and protested enough. He who will not listen to or believe this

commandment may go on until he learns this by experience. Yet it must be impressed upon the young [Deuteronomy 6:7] so that they may be careful not to follow the old lawless crowd, but keep their eyes fixed upon God's commandment, lest His wrath and punishment come upon them
too. It is necessary for us to do no more than to 249
teach and to warn with God's Word. But to check such open greediness there is need for the princes and government. They themselves should take note and have the courage to establish and maintain order in all kinds of trade and commerce. They must do this lest the poor be burdened and oppressed and the leaders themselves be burdened with other people's sins.

This is enough of an explanation of what 250
stealing is. Let the commandment not be understood too narrowly. But let it apply to everything that has to do with our neighbors. Briefly, in summary (as in the former commandments) this is what is forbidden: (a) To do our neighbor any injury or wrong (in any conceivable manner, by impeding, hindering, and withholding his possessions and property), or even to consent or allow such injury. Instead, we should interfere
and prevent it. (b) It is commanded that we ad- 251
vance and improve his possessions. When they suffer lack, we should help, share, and lend both

to friends and foes [Matthew 5:42].

252 Whoever now seeks and desires good works will find here more than enough to do that are heartily acceptable and pleasing to God. In addition, they are favored and crowned with excellent blessings. So we are to be richly compensated for all that we do for our neighbor's good and from friendship. King Solomon also teaches this in Proverbs 19:17, "Whoever is generous to the poor lends to the LORD, and He will repay him for his
253 deed." Here, then, you have a rich Lord. He is certainly enough for you. He will not allow you to come up short in anything or to lack [Psalm 37:25]. So you can with a joyful conscience enjoy a hundred times more than you could scrape together with unfaithfulness and wrong. Now, whoever does not desire this blessing will find enough wrath and misfortune.

THE EIGHTH COMMANDMENT

254 **You shall not bear false witness against your neighbor.**

255 Over and above our own body, spouse, and temporal possessions, we still have another treasure—honor and good reputation [Proverbs

22:1]. We cannot do without these. For it is intolerable to live among people in open shame and
general contempt. Therefore, God does not want 256
the reputation, good name, and upright character
of our neighbor to be taken away or diminished,
just as with his money and possessions. He wants
everyone to stand in his integrity before wife,
children, servants, and neighbors. In the first 257
place, we must consider the plainest meaning of
this commandment, according to the words "You
shall not bear false witness." This applies to the
public courts of justice, where a poor, innocent
man is accused and oppressed by false witnesses
in order to be punished in his body, property, or
honor.

Now, this commandment appears as though 258
it were of little concern to us at present. But with the Jewish people it was a quite common and ordinary matter. For the people were organized under an excellent and regular government. Where there is still such a government, instances of this sin will not be lacking. The cause of it is that where judges, mayors, princes, or others in authority sit in judgment, things never fail to go according to the way of the world. In other words, people do not like to offend anybody. They flatter and speak to gain favor, money, prospects,

or friendship [Proverbs 26:28]. As a result, a poor man and his cause must be oppressed, denounced as wrong, and suffer punishment. It is a common disaster in the world that in courts of justice godly men seldom preside.

259 To be a judge requires above all things a godly man, and not only a godly man, but also a wise, modest, indeed, a brave and bold man. Likewise, to be a witness requires a fearless and especially godly man. For a person who is to judge all matters rightly and carry them through with his decision will often offend good friends, relatives, neighbors, and the rich and powerful, who may greatly serve or injure him. Therefore, he must be quite blind, have his eyes and ears closed, neither see nor hear, but go straight forward in everything that comes before him and decide accordingly.

260 Therefore, this commandment is given in the first place so that everyone shall help his neighbor to secure his rights and not allow them to be hindered or twisted. But everyone shall promote and strictly maintain these rights, no matter whether he is a judge or a witness, and let it apply
261 to whatsoever it will. A particular goal is set up here for our jurists that they be careful to deal truly and uprightly with every case, allowing right

to remain right. On the other hand, they must not pervert anything by their tricks and technical points, turning black into white and making wrong out to be right [Isaiah 5:20]. They must not gloss over a matter or keep silent about it, regardless of a person's money, possession, honor, or power. This is one part and the plainest sense of this commandment about all that takes place in court.

Next, this commandment extends very much 262
further, if we are to apply it to spiritual jurisdiction or administration. Here it is a common occurrence that everyone bears false witness against his neighbor. For wherever there are godly preachers and Christians, they must bear the sentence before the world that calls them heretics, apostates, and indeed, instigators and desperately wicked unbelievers. Besides, God's Word must suffer in the most shameful and hateful manner, being persecuted, blasphemed, contradicted, perverted, and falsely quoted and interpreted. But let this go. For this is the way of the blind world, which condemns and persecutes the truth and God's children, and yet considers it no sin.

In the third place, which concerns us all, this 263
commandment forbids all sins of the tongue

[James 3], by which we may injure or confront our neighbor. To bear false witness is nothing else than a work of the tongue. Now, God prohibits whatever is done with the tongue against a fellow man. This applies to false preachers with their doctrine and blasphemy, false judges and witnesses with their verdict, or outside of court by
264 lying and speaking evil. Here belongs particularly the detestable, shameful vice of speaking behind a person's back and slandering, to which the devil spurs us on, and of which much could be said. For it is a common evil plague that everyone prefers hearing evil more than hearing good about his neighbor. We ourselves are so bad that we cannot allow anyone to say anything bad about us. Everyone would much prefer that all the world should speak of him in glowing terms. Yet we cannot bear that the best is spoken about others.

265 To avoid this vice we should note that no one is allowed publicly to judge and reprove his neighbor—even though he may see him sin—unless he
266 has a command to judge and to reprove. There is a great difference between these two things: judging sin and knowing about sin. You may indeed know about it, but you are not to judge it [Matthew 7:1–5]. I can indeed see and hear that my neighbor sins. But I have no command to report

it to others. Now, if I rush in, judging and passing sentence, I fall into a sin that is greater than his. But if you know about it, do nothing other than turn your ears into a grave and cover it, until you are appointed to be judge and to punish by virtue of your office.

People are called slanderers who are not con- 267
tent with knowing a thing, but go on to assume jurisdiction. When they know about a slight offense committed by another person, they carry it into every corner. They are delighted and tickled that they can stir up another's displeasure, just as swine delight to roll themselves in the dirt and
root in it with the snout. This is nothing other 268
than meddling with God's judgment and office and pronouncing sentence and punishment with the most severe verdict. For no judge can punish to a higher degree nor go farther than to say, "That person is a thief, a murderer, a traitor," and so on. Therefore, whoever presumes to say the same things about his neighbor goes just as far as the emperor and all governments. For although you do not wield the sword, you use your poisonous tongue to shame and hurt your neighbor [Psalm 140:3].

God, therefore, would have such behav- 269
ior banned, that anyone should speak evil of

another person even though that person is guilty, and the latter knows it well, much less if anyone does not know it and has the story only from hearsay.

270 But you say, "Shall I not say something if it is the truth?"

Answer: "Why do you not make your accusation to regular judges?"

"Ah, I cannot prove it publicly, and so I might be silenced and turned away in a harsh manner."

"Ah, indeed, do you smell the roast?"

If you do not trust yourself to stand before the proper authorities and to answer well, then hold your tongue. But if you know about it, know it for yourself and not for another. For if you tell the matter to others—although it is true—you will look like a liar, because you cannot prove it. Besides, you are acting like a rascal. We should never deprive anyone of his honor or good name unless it is first taken away from him publicly.

271 "False witness," then, is everything that can-
272 not be properly proved. No one shall make public or declare for truth what is not obvious by sufficient evidence. In short, whatever is secret should be allowed to remain secret [1 Peter 4:8], or, at any rate, should be secretly rebuked, as we shall

hear. Therefore, if you meet an idle tongue that betrays and slanders someone, contradict such a person promptly to his face [Proverbs 10:31], so he may blush. Then many a person will hold his tongue who otherwise would bring some poor man into bad repute, from which he would not easily free himself. For honor and a good name are easily taken away, but not easily restored [Proverbs 22:1]. 273

So you see that it is directly forbidden to speak any evil of our neighbor. However, the civil government, preachers, father, and mother are not forbidden to speak out. This is based on the understanding that this commandment does not allow evil to go unpunished. Now, in the Fifth Commandment no one is to be injured in body, and yet Master Hans (the executioner) is excluded from this rule. By virtue of his office he does his neighbor no good, but only evil and harm. Nevertheless he does not sin against God's commandment. God has instituted that office on His own account. God has reserved punishment for His own good pleasure, as He threatens in the First Commandment. In the same way, although no one has a personal right to judge and condemn anybody, yet if those who serve in offices of judgment fail to judge, they sin just as surely as a 274

person who would act on his own accord without such an office. For in matters of justice necessity requires one to speak of the evil, to prefer charges,
275 to investigate, and to testify. This is no different from the case of a doctor who is sometimes compelled to examine and handle the private parts of the patient whom he is to cure. In the same way governments, father and mother, brothers and sisters, and other good friends are under obligation to one another to rebuke evil wherever it is needful and profitable [Luke 17:3].

276 The true way in this matter would be to keep the order in the Gospel. In Matthew 18:15, Christ says, "If your brother sins against you, go and tell him his fault, between you and him alone." Here you have a precious and excellent teaching for governing well the tongue, which is to be carefully kept against this detestable misuse. Let this, then, be your rule, that you do not too quickly spread evil about your neighbor and slander him to others. Instead, admonish him privately that he may amend his life. Likewise, if someone reports to you what this or that person has done, teach him, too, to go and admonish that person personally, if he has seen the deed himself. But if he has not seen it, then let him hold his tongue.

277 You can learn the same thing also from the

daily government of the household. When the master of the house sees that the servant does not do what he ought, he admonishes him personally. But if he were so foolish as to let the servant sit at home and went on the streets to complain about him to his neighbors, he would no doubt
be told, "You fool, how does that concern us? 278
Why don't you tell it to the servant?" Look, that would be acting quite brotherly, so that the evil would be stopped, and your neighbor would retain his honor. As Christ also says in the same place, "If he listens to you, you have gained your brother" [Matthew 18:15]. Then you have done a great and excellent work. For do you think it is a small matter to gain a brother? Let all monks and holy orders step forth, with all their works melted together into one mass, and see if they can boast that they have gained a brother.

Further, Christ teaches, "But if he does not 279
listen, take one or two others along with you, that every charge may be established by the evidence of two or three witnesses" [Matthew 18:16]. So the person concerned in this matter must always be dealt with personally, and must
not be spoken of without his knowledge. But if 280
that does not work, then bring it publicly before the community, whether before the civil or the

Church court. For then you do not stand alone, but you have those witnesses with you by whom you can convict the guilty one. Relying on their testimony the judge can pronounce sentence and punish. This is the right and regular course for
281 checking and reforming a wicked person. But if we gossip about another in all corners, and stir the filth, no one will be reformed. Later, when we are to stand up and bear witness, we deny having
282 said so. Therefore, it would serve such tongues right if their itch for slander were severely pun-
283 ished, as a warning to others. If you were acting for your neighbor's reformation or from love of the truth, you would not sneak about secretly nor shun the day and the light [John 3:19–20].

284 All this has been said about secret sins. But where the sin is quite public, so that the judge and everybody know about it, you can without any sin shun the offender and let him go his own way, because he has brought himself into disgrace. You may also publicly testify about him. For when a matter is public in the daylight, there can be no slandering or false judging or testifying. It is like when we now rebuke the pope with his doctrine, which is publicly set forth in books and proclaimed in all the world. Where the sin is public, the rebuke also must be public, that everyone may learn to guard against it.

Now we have the sum and general under- 285
standing of this commandment: Let no one do any harm to his neighbor with the tongue, whether friend or foe. Do not speak evil of him, no matter whether it is true or false, unless it is done by commandment or for his reformation. Let everyone use his tongue and make it serve for the best of everyone else, to cover up his neighbor's sins and infirmities [1 Peter 4:8], excuse them, conceal
and garnish them with his own reputation. The 286
chief reason for this should be the one that Christ declares in the Gospel, where He includes all commandments about our neighbor, "whatever you wish that others would do to you, do also to them" [Matthew 7:12].

Even nature teaches the same thing in our 287
own bodies, as St. Paul says, "On the contrary, the parts of the body that seem to be weaker are indispensable, and on those parts of the body that we think less honorable we bestow the greater honor, and our unpresentable parts are treated with greater modesty" (1 Corinthians 12:22–23). No one covers his face, eyes, nose, and mouth, for they, being in themselves the most honorable parts that we have, do not require it. But the most weak parts, of which we are ashamed, we cover with all diligence. Hands, eyes, and the whole body must help to cover and conceal

288 them. So also among ourselves should we clothe
whatever blemishes and infirmities we find in
our neighbor and serve and help him to promote
his honor to the best of our ability. On the other
hand, we should prevent whatever may be dis-
289 graceful to him. It is especially an excellent and
noble virtue for someone always to explain things
for his neighbor's advantage and to put the best
construction on all he may hear about his neighbor (if it is not notoriously evil). Or, at any rate,
forgive the matter over and against the poisonous
tongues that are busy wherever they can to pry
out and discover something to blame in a neighbor [Psalm 140:3]. They explain and pervert the
matter in the worst way, as is done now especially
with God's precious Word and its preachers.

290 There are included, therefore, in this commandment quite a multitude of good works.
These please God most highly and bring abundant good and blessing, if only the blind world
291 and the false saints would recognize them. For
there is nothing on or in a person that can do
both greater and more extensive good or harm
in spiritual and in temporal matters than the
tongue. This is true even though it is the least and
weakest part of a person [James 3:5].

THE NINTH AND TENTH COMMANDMENTS

You shall not covet your neighbor's house. 292

You shall not covet your neighbor's wife, or his manservant, or his maidservant, or his cattle, or anything that is his.

These two commandments are given quite 293
exclusively to the Jewish people. Nevertheless, in part they also apply to us. For they do not interpret them as referring to unchastity or theft. These are forbidden well enough above. They also thought that they had kept all those commands when they had done or not done the external act. Therefore, God has added these two commandments in order that it be considered sinful and forbidden to desire or in any way to aim at
getting our neighbor's wife or possessions. He 294
added them especially because under the Jewish government manservants and maidservants were not free as now to serve for wages as long as they pleased. Jewish servants were their master's property with their body and all they had, as were cattle and other possessions [Deuteronomy
15:12–18]. Further, every man had power over 295
his wife to put her away publicly by giving her a

bill of divorce and to take another [Deuteronomy 24:1–4]. Therefore, they were in constant danger among each other. If one took a fancy to another's wife, he might declare any reason both to dismiss his own wife and to estrange his neighbor's wife from him, so that he might get her in a way that appeared right. That was not considered a sin or a disgrace among them, just as it is hardly considered a sin now with hired help, when an owner dismisses his manservant or maidservant or takes another's servants from him in any way.

296 In this way they interpreted these commandments, and that rightly (although the scope of the commandment reaches somewhat farther and higher). No one should consider or intend to get what belongs to another, such as his wife, servants, house and estate, land, meadows, cattle. He should not take them even with a show of right, by a trick, or to his neighbor's harm. For above, in the Seventh Commandment, the vice is forbidden where one takes for himself the possessions of others or withholds them from his neighbor. A person cannot rightly do these things. But here it is also forbidden for you to alienate anything from your neighbor, even though you could do so with honor in the eyes of the world, so that no one could accuse or blame you as though you had gotten it wrongfully.

For our natural instinct is that no one wants to 297
see someone else have as much as himself. Each
one acquires as much as he can. The other may do
as best he can. Yet we pretend to be godly, know 298
how to dress ourselves up most finely, and conceal our base character. We resort to and invent tricky ways and deceitful works (like those that are now daily and most ingeniously invented). We act as though these ways were derived from the legal codes. In fact, we even dare properly to refer to the law and boast about it. We will not have this called trickery, but shrewdness and cau-
tion. Lawyers and jurists assist in this who twist 299
and stretch the law to suit it to their cause. They stress words and use them for a trick, despite fairness or their neighbor's need. In short, whoever is the most expert and cunning in these affairs finds the most help in the law, as they themselves say, "The laws favor the watchful."

This last commandment, therefore, is given 300
not for cheaters in the eyes of the world. It is for the most pious, who want to be praised and to be called honest and upright people. For they have not offended against the former commandments, as especially the Jewish people claimed to live, and are even now many great noblemen, gentlemen, and princes. For the other common masses belong yet further down, under the Seventh

Commandment, as people who are hardly concerned about whether they gain their possessions with honor and right.

301 Now, this happens most often in cases that are brought into court, where it is the purpose to get something from our neighbor and to force him from his property. For example, when people quarrel and wrangle about a large inheritance, real estate, or such, they help themselves and resort to whatever appears right. They dress and adorn everything so that the law must favor their side. They keep the property with such title
302 that no one can complain or lay claim to it. In the same way, if anyone wants to have a castle, city, duchy, or any other great thing, he makes many financial deals through relationships, by any means he can, so that the owner is legally deprived of the property [1 Kings 21]. It is awarded to the other person and confirmed with deed and seal and declared to have been acquired by princely title and honesty.

303 In common trade, one carefully slips something out of another's hand, so that the latter must watch out. Or one person surprises and cheats another in a matter where he sees advantage and benefit for himself. Then the person who was cheated, perhaps on account of distress

or debt, cannot regain or redeem the property without damage. The other person gains the half or even more. Yet this property must not be considered as taken by fraud or stolen, but honestly bought. Here they say, "First come, first served," and "Everyone must look to his own interest, let another get what he can." Who can be so smart 304
to come up with all these ways in which one can get many things into his possession by such believable arguments? The world does not consider this wrong and will not notice that the neighbor is placed at a disadvantage by this, by sacrificing what he cannot spare without harm. Yet no one wishes for someone to do this to himself. From this we can easily see that such devices and arguments are false.

The same was done in former times also with 305
respect to wives. They knew such tricks, that if one were pleased with another woman, he personally or through others (as there were many ways and means to be invented) caused her husband to become displeased with her. Or he had her resist her husband and act in such a way that he was obliged to dismiss her and let her go to the other man. That sort of thing undoubtedly prevailed much under the Law, as we also read in the Gospel about King Herod. He took his brother's wife while he

was still living. Yet Herod wanted to be thought of as an honorable, pious man, as St. Mark also
306 testifies about him [Mark 6:17–20]. But such an example, I trust, will not happen among us. For in the New Testament those who are married are forbidden to get divorced [Mark 10:9]. (Except there is the case where one man shrewdly by some trick takes away a rich bride from another man.) But it is not a rare thing with us that one estranges or alienates another's manservant or maidservant or lures them away with flattering words.

307 In whatever way such things happen, we must know that God does not want you to deprive your neighbor of anything that belongs to him, so that he suffer the loss and you gratify your greed with it. This is true even if you could keep it honorably before the world. For it is a secret and sly trick done "under the hat," as we say, so it may not be noticed. Although you go your way as if you had done no one any wrong, you have still injured your neighbor. If it is not called stealing and cheating, it is still called coveting your neighbor's property, that is, aiming at possession of it, luring it away from him without his consent, and being unwilling to see him enjoy
308 what God has granted him. Even though the judge and everyone must let you keep it, God

will not let you keep it. For He sees the deceitful heart and world's malice, which is sure to take an extra long measure wherever you yield to her a finger's breadth. Eventually public wrong and violence follow.

Therefore, we allow these commandments 309
to remain in their ordinary meaning. It is commanded, first, that we do not desire our neighbor's harm, nor even assist, nor give opportunity for it. But we must gladly wish and leave him what he has. Also, we must advance and preserve for him what may be for his profit and service, just as we wish to be treated [Matthew 7:12].
So these commandments are especially directed 310
against envy and miserable greed. God wants to remove all causes and sources from which arises everything by which we harm our neighbor. Therefore, He expresses it in plain words, "You shall not covet," and so on. For He especially wants us to have a pure heart [Matthew 5:8], although we will never attain to that as long as we live here. So this commandment will remain, like all the rest, one that will constantly accuse us and show how godly we are in God's sight!

CONCLUSION OF THE TEN COMMANDMENTS

311 Now we have the Ten Commandments, a summary of divine teaching about what we are to do in order that our whole life may be pleasing to God. Everything that is to be a good work must arise and flow from and in this true fountain and channel. So apart from the Ten Commandments no work or thing can be good or pleasing to God, no matter how great or precious it is in the
312 world's eyes. Let us see now what our great saints can boast of their spiritual orders and their great and mighty works. They have invented and set these things up, while they let these commandments go, as though they were far too insignificant or had long ago been perfectly fulfilled.

313 I am of the opinion, indeed, that here one will find his hands full ‹and will have enough› to do to keep these commandments: meekness, patience, love towards enemies, chastity, kindness, and other such virtues and their implications [Galatians 5:22–23]. But such works are not of value and make no display in the world's eyes. For these are not peculiar and proud works. They are not restricted to particular times, places, rites, and customs. They

are common, everyday, household works that one neighbor can do for another. Therefore, they are not highly regarded.

But the other works cause people to open 314
their eyes and ears wide. Men aid this effect by the great display, expense, and magnificent buildings with which they adorn such works, so that everything shines and glitters. There they waft incense, they sing and ring bells, they light tapers and candles, so that nothing else can be seen or heard. For when a priest stands there in a surplice garment embroidered with gold thread, or a layman continues all day upon his knees in Church, that is regarded as a most precious work, which no one can praise enough. But when a poor girl tends a little child and faithfully does what she is told, that is considered nothing. For what else should monks and nuns seek in their cloisters?

Look, is not this a cursed overconfidence 315
of those desperate saints who dare to invent a higher and better life and estate than the Ten Commandments teach? To pretend (as we have said) that this is an ordinary life for the common man, but theirs is for saints and perfect
ones? The miserable blind people do not see 316
that no person can go far enough to keep one of the Ten Commandments as it should be

kept. Both the Apostles' Creed and the Lord's Prayer must come to our aid (as we shall hear). By them ‹power and strength to keep the commandments› is sought and prayed for and received continually. Therefore, all their boasting amounts to as much as if I boasted and said, "To be sure, I don't have a penny to make payment with, but I confidently will try to pay ten florins."

317 All this I say and teach so that people might get rid of the sad misuse that has taken such deep root and still clings to everybody. In all estates upon earth they must get used to looking at these commandments only and to be concerned about these matters. For it will be a long time before they will produce a teaching or estate equal to the Ten Commandments, because they are so high that no one can reach them by human power. Whoever does reach them is a heavenly, angelic person, far above all holiness
318 of the world. Just occupy yourself with them. Try your best. Apply all power and ability. You will find so much to do that you will neither seek nor value any other work or holiness.

319 Let this be enough about the first part of the common Christian doctrine, both for teaching and urging what is necessary. In conclusion,

however, we must repeat the text which belongs here. We have presented this already in the First Commandment, in order that we may learn what pains God requires so that we may learn to teach and do the Ten Commandments:

> For I the Lord your God am a jealous God, visiting the iniquity of the fathers on the children to the third and the fourth generation of those who hate Me, but showing steadfast love to thousands of those who love Me and keep My commandments. [Exodus 20:5–6] 320

As we have heard above, this appendix was primarily attached to the First Commandment. Yet it was laid down for the sake of all the commandments, since all of them are to be referred and directed to it. Therefore, I have said that this also should be presented to and taught to the young. Then they may learn and remember it, and we may see what must move and compel us to keep these Ten Commandments. This part is to be regarded as though it were specially added to each command, so that it dwells in, and runs through, them all. 321

Now, there is included in these words (as said before) both an angry, threatening word and a friendly promise. These are to terrify and warn us. They are also to lead and encourage us to receive 322

and highly value His Word as a matter of divine sincerity. For God Himself declares how much He is concerned about it and how rigidly He will enforce it: He will horribly and terribly punish all who despise and transgress His commandments.
323 Also, He declares how richly He will reward, bless, and do all good to those who hold them in high value and gladly do and live according to them. So God demands that all our works proceed from a heart that fears and regards God alone. From such fear the heart avoids everything that is contrary to His will, lest it should move Him to wrath. And, on the other hand, the heart also trusts in Him alone and from love for Him does all He wants. For He speaks to us as friendly as a father and offers us all grace and every good.

324 This is exactly the meaning and true interpretation of the first and chief commandment, from which all the others must flow and proceed. So this word, "You shall have no other gods before Me" [Exodus 20:3], in its simplest meaning states nothing other than this demand: You shall fear, love, and trust in Me as your only true God. For where there is a heart set in this way before God, that heart has fulfilled this commandment and all the other commandments. On the other hand, whoever fears and loves anything else in heaven

and upon earth will keep neither this nor any of the commandments. So then all the Scriptures 325
have everywhere preached and taught this commandment, aiming always at these two things: fear of God and trust in Him. The prophet David especially does this throughout the Psalms, as when he says "the LORD takes pleasure in those who fear Him, in those who hope in His steadfast love" [Psalm 147:11]. He writes as if the entire commandment were explained by one verse, as if to say, "The Lord takes pleasure in those who have no other gods."

So the First Commandment is to shine and 326
give its splendor to all the others. Therefore, you must let this declaration run through all the commandments. It is like a hoop in a wreath, joining the end to the beginning and holding them all together. Let it be continually repeated and not forgotten, as the Second Commandment says, so that we fear God and do not take His name in vain for cursing, lying, deceiving, and other ways of leading men astray, or trickery. But we make proper and good use of His name by calling upon Him in prayer, praise, and thanksgiving, derived from love and trust according to the First Commandment. In the same way such fear, love, and trust is to drive and force us not to despise His

Word, but gladly to learn it, hear it, value it holy, and honor it.

327 So this teaching continues through all the following commandments toward our neighbor. Everything is to flow from the First Commandment's power. We honor father and mother, masters, and all in authority, and are subject and obedient to them, not for their own sake, but for God's sake. You are not to regard or fear father or mother, nor should you do or skip anything because you love them. But note what God would have you do, what He will quite surely demand of you. If you skip that, you have an angry Judge. But if you do the work, you have a gracious Father.

328 Again, do your neighbor no harm, injury, or violence, nor in any way oppress him with regard to his body, wife, property, honor, or rights. All these things are commanded in their order, even though you may have a chance and cause to do wrong and no person would rebuke you. But do good to all men [Galatians 6:10]. Help them and promote their interest—in every way and wherever you can—purely out of love for God and to please Him. Do this in the confidence that He will abundantly reward you for everything.
329 Now you see how the First Commandment is

the chief source and fountainhead that flows into all the rest. Note again, all return to that First Commandment and depend upon it. So beginning and end are fastened and bound to each other.

This is always profitable and necessary to teach 330
to the young people. Admonish them and remind them of it, so that they may be brought up not only with blows and compulsion, like cattle, but in the fear and reverence of God. Let this be considered and laid to heart that these things are not human games, but are the commandments of the Divine Majesty. He insists on them with great seriousness. He is angry with and punishes those who despise them. On the other hand, He abundantly rewards those who keep them. In this way there will be a spontaneous drive and a desire gladly
to do God's will. Therefore, it is not meaningless 331
that it is commanded in the Old Testament that we should write the Ten Commandments on all walls and corners, yes, even on our garments [Deuteronomy 6:8–9]. This is not for the sake of merely having them written in these places and making a show of them. The Jewish people did that. But it is so we might have our eyes constantly fixed on them. We should have them always in our memory. Then we might do them in all our

332 actions and ways. Then everyone may make them his daily exercise in all cases, in every business and transaction, as though they were written in every place wherever he would look, indeed, wherever he walks or stands. Then there would be enough opportunity—both at home in our own house and abroad with our neighbors—to do the Ten Commandments, so that no one would need to run far to find them.

333 From this it again appears how highly these Ten Commandments are to be exalted and extolled above all estates, commandments, and works that are taught and done apart from them. For here we can boast and say, "Let all the wise people and saints step forth and produce, if they can, a single work like these commandments. God insists on these with such seriousness. He commands them with His greatest wrath and punishment. Besides, He adds such glorious promises to them that He will pour out upon us all good things and blessings. Therefore, they should be taught above all others and be valued precious and dear, as the highest treasure given by God."

PART 2

THE APOSTLES' CREED

So far we have heard the first part of Christian 1
doctrine. We have seen all that God wants us to
do or not to do. Now there properly follows the
Creed, which sets forth to us everything that we
must expect and receive from God. To state it quite
briefly, the Creed teaches us to know Him fully
[Ephesians 3:19]. This is intended to help us do 2
what we ought to do according to the Ten Commandments. For (as said above) the Ten Commandments are set so high that all human ability
is far too feeble and weak to keep them. Therefore,
it is just as necessary to learn this part of Christian
doctrine as to learn the former. Then we may know
how to attain what they command, both where and
how to receive such power. For if we could by our 3
own powers keep the Ten Commandments as they
should be kept, we would need nothing further,
neither the Creed nor the Lord's Prayer. But be- 4
fore we explain this advantage and necessity of the
Creed, it is enough at first for the simpleminded
to learn to comprehend and understand the Creed
itself.

In the first place, the Creed has until now 5

been divided into twelve articles. Yet, if all the doctrinal points that are written in the Scriptures and that belong to the Creed were to be distinctly set forth, there would be far more articles. They could not all be clearly expressed in so few words.
6 But to make the Creed most easily and clearly understood as it is to be taught to children, we shall briefly sum up the entire Creed in three chief articles, according to the three persons in the Godhead [Colossians 2:9]. Everything that we believe is related to these three persons. So the First Article, about God the Father, explains creation. The Second Article, about the Son, explains redemption. And the Third, about the Holy
7 Spirit, explains sanctification. We present them as though the Creed were briefly summarized in so many words: I believe in God the Father, who has created me; I believe in God the Son, who has redeemed me; I believe in the Holy Spirit, who sanctifies me. One God and one faith, but three persons. Therefore, three articles or confessions.
8 Let us go over the words briefly.

ARTICLE I

9

I believe in God the Father Almighty, maker of heaven and earth.

This shows and sets forth most briefly what 10
is God the Father's essence, will, activity, and work. The Ten Commandments have taught that we are to have not more than one God [Deuteronomy 6:4]. So it might be asked, "What kind of a person is God? What does He do? How can we praise, or show and describe Him, that He may be known?" Now, that is taught in this and in the following article. So the Creed is nothing other than the answer and confession of Christians arranged with respect to the First Commandment.
It is as if you were to ask a little child, "My dear, 11
what sort of a God do you have? What do you know about Him?" The child could say, "This is my God: first, the Father, who has created heaven and earth. Besides this One only, I regard nothing else as God. For there is no one else who could create heaven and earth."

But for the learned and those who are some- 12
what advanced, these three articles may all be expanded and divided into as many parts as there are words. But now for young scholars let it suffice to make the most necessary points, as we have said, that this article refers to the Creation. We emphasize the words "Creator of heaven and
earth." But what is the force of this, or what do 13
you mean by these words, "I believe in God the

Father Almighty, maker of heaven and earth?"
Answer: "This is what I mean and believe, that
I am God's creature [2 Corinthians 5:17]. I
mean that He has given and constantly preserves
[Psalm 36:6] for me my body, soul, and life, my
members great and small, all my senses, reason,
and understanding, and so on. He gives me
food and drink, clothing and support, wife and
children, domestic servants, house and home,
14 and more. Besides, He causes all created things
to serve for the uses and necessities of life. These
include the sun, moon, and stars in the heavens,
day and night, air, fire, water, earth, and whatever
it bears and produces. They include birds and
fish, beasts, grain, and all kinds of produce [Psalm
15 104]. They also include whatever else there is for
bodily and temporal goods, like good govern-
16 ment, peace, and security." So we learn from this
article that none of us owns for himself, nor can
preserve, his life nor anything that is here listed
or can be listed. This is true no matter how small
and unimportant a thing it might be. For all is
included in the word *Creator*.

17 Further, we also confess that God the Father has not only given us all that we have and see before our eyes, but He daily preserves and defends us against all evil and misfortune [Psalm 5:11].

He directs all sorts of danger and disaster away from us. We confess that He does all this out of pure love and goodness, without our merit, as a kind Father. He cares for us so that no evil falls
upon us. But to speak more about this belongs in 18
the other two parts of this article, where we say, "Father Almighty."

19 Now, all that we have, and whatever else is in heaven and upon the earth, is daily given, preserved, and kept for us by God. Therefore, it is clearly suggested and concluded that it is our duty to love, praise, and thank Him for these things without ceasing [1 Thessalonians 5:17–18]. In short, we should serve Him with all these things, as He demands and has taught in the Ten Commandments.

20 We could say much here, if we were to wander, about how few people believe this article. For we all pass over it, hear it, and say it. Yet we do not see or consider what the words teach us.
For if we believed this teaching with the heart, we 21
would also act according to it [James 2:14]. We would not strut about proudly, act defiantly, and boast as though we had life, riches, power, honor, and such, of ourselves [James 4:13–16]. We would not act as though others must fear and serve us, as is the practice of the wretched, perverse world.

The world is drowned in blindness and abuses all the good things and God's gifts only for its own pride, greed, lust, and luxury. It never once thinks about God, so as to thank Him or acknowledge Him as Lord and Creator.

22 This article ought to humble and terrify us all, if we believed it. For we sin daily [Hebrews 3:12–13] with eyes, ears, hands, body and soul, money and possessions, and with everything we have. This is especially true of those who fight against God's Word. Yet Christians have this advantage: they acknowledge that they are duty bound to serve God for all these things and to be obedient to Him.

23 We ought, therefore, daily to recite this article. We ought to impress it upon our mind and remember it by all that meets our eyes and by all good that falls to us. Wherever we escape from disaster or danger, we ought to remember that it is God who gives and does all these things. In these escapes we sense and see His fatherly heart and His surpassing love toward us [Exodus 34:6]. In this way the heart would be warmed and kindled to be thankful, and to use all such good things to honor and praise God.

24 We have most briefly presented the meaning of this article. This is how much is necessary at

first for the most simple to learn about what we have, what we receive from God, and what we owe in return. This is a most excellent knowledge but a far greater treasure. For here we see how the Father has given Himself to us, together with all creatures, and has most richly provided for us in this life. We see that He has overwhelmed us with unspeakable, eternal treasures by His Son and the Holy Spirit, as we shall hear [Colossians 2:2].

ARTICLE II

And in Jesus Christ, His only Son, our Lord, who was conceived by the Holy Spirit, born of the virgin Mary, suffered under Pontius Pilate, was crucified, died and was buried. He descended into hell. The third day He rose again from the dead. He ascended into heaven and sits at the right hand of God the Father Almighty. From thence He will come to judge the living and the dead. 25

Here we learn to know the Second Person of the Godhead. We see what we have from God over and above the temporal goods mentioned before. We see how He has completely poured forth Himself [Matthew 26:28] and withheld nothing from us [2 Corinthians 8:9]. Now, this 26 article is very rich and broad. But in order to explain it briefly also and in a childlike way, we shall take up one phrase and sum up the entire article. As we have said, we may learn from this article how we have been redeemed. We shall base this on these words, "In Jesus Christ, our Lord."

27 Now, if you are asked, "What do you believe in the Second Article about Jesus Christ?" answer briefly,

"I believe that Jesus Christ, God's true Son, has become my Lord."

"But what does it mean to become Lord?"

"It is this. He has redeemed me from sin, from the devil, from death, and from all evil. For before I did not have a Lord or King, but was captive under the devil's power, condemned to death, stuck in sin and blindness" [see Ephesians 2:1–3].

28 For when we had been created by God the Father and had received from Him all kinds of good, the devil came and led us into disobedience, sin, death, and all evil [Genesis 3]. So we fell under God's wrath and displeasure and were doomed to eternal damnation, just as we had
29 merited and deserved. There was no counsel, help, or comfort until this only and eternal Son of God—in His immeasurable goodness—had

compassion upon our misery and wretchedness.
He came from heaven to help us [John 1:9]. So 30
those tyrants and jailers are all expelled now. In their place has come Jesus Christ, Lord of life, righteousness, every blessing, and salvation. He has delivered us poor, lost people from hell's jaws, has won us, has made us free [Romans 8:1–2], and has brought us again into the Father's favor and grace. He has taken us as His own property under His shelter and protection [Psalm 61:3–4] so that He may govern us by His righteousness, wisdom, power, life, and blessedness.

Let this, then, be the sum of this article: the 31
little word *Lord* means simply the same as *redeemer.* It means the One who has brought us from Satan to God, from death to life, from sin to righteousness, and who preserves us in the same. But all the points that follow in this article serve no other purpose than to explain and express this redemption. They explain how and by whom it was accomplished. They explain how much it cost Him and what He spent and risked so that He might win us and bring us under His dominion. It explains that He became man [John 1:14], was conceived and born without sin [Hebrews 4:15], from the Holy Spirit and from the virgin Mary [Luke 1:35], so that He might overcome sin.

Further, it explains that He suffered, died, and was buried so that He might make satisfaction for me and pay what I owe [1 Corinthians 15:3–4], not with silver or gold, but with His own precious blood [1 Peter 1:18–19]. And He did all this in order to become my Lord. He did none of these things for Himself, nor did He have any need for redemption. After that He rose again from the dead, swallowed up and devoured death [1 Corinthians 15:54], and finally ascended into heaven and assumed the government at the Father's right hand [1 Peter 3:22]. He did these things so that the devil and all powers must be subject to Him and lie at His feet [Hebrews 10:12–13] until finally, at the Last Day, He will completely divide and separate us from the wicked world, the devil, death, sin, and such [Matthew 25:31–46; 13:24–30, 47–50].

32 To explain all these individual points does not belong to brief sermons for children. That belongs to fuller sermons that extend throughout the entire year, especially at those times that are appointed for the purpose of treating each article at length—for Christ's birth, sufferings, resurrection, ascension, and so on.

33 Yes, the entire Gospel that we preach is based on this point, that we properly understand this

article as that upon which our salvation and all our happiness rests. It is so rich and complete that we can never learn it fully.

ARTICLE III

I believe in the Holy Spirit, the holy Christian 34
Church, the communion of saints, the forgiveness of sins, the resurrection of the body, and the life everlasting. Amen.

I cannot connect this article (as I have said) to 35
anything better than Sanctification. Through this
article the Holy Spirit, with His office, is declared
and shown: He makes people holy [1 Corinthians
6:11]. Therefore, we must take our stand upon
the term *Holy Spirit*, because it is so precise and
complete that we cannot find another. For there 36
are many kinds of spirits mentioned in the Holy
Scriptures, such as the spirit of man [1 Corinthians 2:11], heavenly spirits [Hebrews 12:23], and
evil spirits [Luke 7:21]. But God's Spirit alone is
called the Holy Spirit, that is, He who has sanctified and still sanctifies us. For just as the Father
is called "Creator" and the Son is called "Redeemer," so the Holy Spirit, from His work, must
be called "Sanctifier," or "One who makes holy."

"But how is such sanctifying done?" 37

Answer, "The Son receives dominion, by which He wins us, through His birth, death, resurrection, and so on. In a similar way, the Holy Spirit causes our sanctification by the following: the communion of saints or the Christian Church, the forgiveness of sins, the resurrection of the body, and the life everlasting. That means He leads us first into His holy congregation and places us in the bosom of the Church. Through the Church He preaches to us and brings us to Christ."

38 Neither you nor I could ever know anything about Christ, or believe on Him, and have Him for our Lord, unless it were offered to us and granted to our hearts by the Holy Spirit through the preaching of the Gospel [1 Corinthians 12:3; Galatians 4:6]. The work of redemption is done and accomplished [John 19:30]. Christ has acquired and gained the treasure for us by His suffering, death, resurrection, and so on [Colossians 2:3]. But if the work remained concealed so that no one knew about it, then it would be useless and lost. So that this treasure might not stay buried, but be received and enjoyed, God has caused the Word to go forth and be proclaimed. In the Word He has the Holy Spirit bring this
39 treasure home and make it our own. Therefore,

sanctifying is just bringing us to Christ so we receive this good, which we could not get ourselves [1 Peter 3:18].

Learn, then, to understand this article most 40
clearly. You may be asked, "What do you mean by the words *I believe in the Holy Spirit*?"

You can then answer, "I believe that the Holy Spirit makes me holy, as His name implies."

"But how does He accomplish this, or what are 41
His method and means to this end?"

Answer, "By the Christian Church, the forgiveness of sins, the resurrection of the body, and
the life everlasting. For in the first place, the Spirit 42
has His own congregation in the world, which is the mother that conceives and bears every Christian through God's Word [Galatians 4:26]. Through the Word He reveals and preaches, He illumines and enkindles hearts, so that they understand, accept, cling to, and persevere in the Word" [1 Corinthians 2:12].

Where the Spirit does not cause the Word to 43
be preached and roused in the heart so that it is understood, it is lost [Matthew 13:19]. This was the case under the papacy, where faith was entirely put under the bench. No one recognized Christ as his Lord or the Holy Spirit as his Sanctifier. That is, no one believed that Christ is our Lord

in the sense that He has gained this treasure for us, without our works and merit [Romans 4:6],
44 and made us acceptable to the Father. What, then, was lacking? This: the Holy Spirit was not there to reveal it and cause it to be preached. But men and evil spirits were there. They taught us to
45 obtain grace and be saved by our works. There is no Christian Church in that. For where Christ is not preached, there is no Holy Spirit who creates, calls, and gathers the Christian Church, without which no one can come to Christ the Lord.

46 Let this be enough about the sum of this article. But since the parts that are numbered here are not quite clear to the simple, we shall go over them also.

47 The Creed calls the "holy Christian Church" a "communion of saints." Both expressions, taken together, are identical. But in the past the expression "communion of saints" was not there. This phrase has been poorly and unwisely translated into the German as a *communion* of saints. If it is to be rendered plainly, it must be expressed quite differently in a German way. In the same way, the word *ecclesia* properly means in German
48 "a gathering." But we are used to seeing it translated as the word *Church,* by which the simple do not understand a gathered multitude but the

consecrated house or building. This is true even though the house ought not to be called a Church, just because the multitude gathers there. For we who gather there make and choose for ourselves a particular place and give a name to the house according to the gathering.

So the word *Church* really means nothing other than a common gathering, and is not really German, but Greek (as is also the word *ecclesia*). For in their own language the Greeks call it *kyria*, as in Latin it is called *curia*. Therefore, in real German, in our mother tongue, it ought to be called "a Christian congregation or gathering" or, best of all and most clearly, "holy Christendom."

So also the word *communio*, which is added, 49
ought not to be translated "communion," but
"congregation." It is nothing else than an interpretation or explanation by which someone
meant to show what the Christian Church is. Our
people understood neither Latin nor German.
They have translated this word "communion of
saints," although no German dialect says this or
understands it this way. But to speak correct German, it ought to be "a congregation of saints"; that
is, a congregation made up purely of saints, or, to
speak yet more plainly, "a holy congregation." I 50
say this in order that the words "communion of

saints" may be understood. The expression has become so established by custom that it cannot be cast aside easily, and it is treated almost as heresy if someone attempts to change a word.

51 But this is the meaning and substance of this addition: I believe that there is upon earth a little holy group and congregation of pure saints, under one head, even Christ [Ephesians 1:22]. This group is called together by the Holy Spirit in one faith, one mind, and understanding, with many different gifts, yet agreeing in love, without
52 sects or schisms [Ephesians 4:5–8, 11]. I am also a part and member of this same group, a sharer and joint owner of all the goods it possesses [Romans 8:17]. I am brought to it and incorporated into it by the Holy Spirit through having heard and continuing to hear God's Word [Galatians 3:1–2], which is the beginning of entering it. In the past, before we had attained to this, we were altogether of the devil, knowing nothing about God and
53 about Christ [Romans 3:10–12]. So, until the Last Day, the Holy Spirit abides with the holy congregation or Christendom [John 14:17]. Through this congregation He brings us to Christ and He teaches and preaches to us the Word [John 14:26]. By the Word He works and promotes sanctification, causing this congregation daily to

grow and to become strong in the faith and its fruit, which He produces [Galatians 5].

We further believe that in this Christian Church we have forgiveness of sin, which is wrought through the holy Sacraments and Absolution [Matthew 26:28; Mark 1:4; John 20:23] and through all kinds of comforting promises from the entire Gospel. Therefore, whatever ought to be preached about the Sacraments belongs here. In short, the whole Gospel and all the offices of Christianity belong here, which also must be preached and taught without ceasing. God's grace is secured through Christ [John 1:17], and sanctification is wrought by the Holy Spirit through God's Word in the unity of the Christian Church. Yet because of our flesh, which we bear about with us, we are never without sin [Romans 7:23–24]. 54

Everything, therefore, in the Christian Church is ordered toward this goal: we shall daily receive in the Church nothing but the forgiveness of sin through the Word and signs, to comfort and encourage our consciences as long as we live here. So even though we have sins, the ‹grace of the› Holy Spirit does not allow them to harm us. For we are in the Christian Church, where there is nothing but ‹continuous, uninterrupted› 55 forgiveness of sin. This is because God forgives us and because we forgive, bear with, and help one another [Galatians 6:1–2].

56 But outside of this Christian Church, where the Gospel is not found, there is no forgiveness, as also there can be no holiness. Therefore, all who seek and wish to earn holiness not through the Gospel and forgiveness of sin, but by their works, have expelled and severed themselves ‹from this Church› [Galatians 5:4].

57 However, while sanctification has begun and
is growing daily [2 Thessalonians 1:3], we expect
that our flesh will be destroyed and buried with
all its uncleanness [Romans 6:4–11]. Then we will
come forth gloriously and arise in a new, eternal
58 life of entire and perfect holiness. For now we are
only half pure and holy. So the Holy Spirit always has some reason to continue His work in us through the Word. He must daily administer forgiveness until we reach the life to come. At that time there will be no more forgiveness, but only perfectly pure and holy people [1 Corinthians 13:10]. We will be full of godliness and righteousness, removed and free from sin, death, and all evil, in a new, immortal, and glorified body [1 Corinthians 15:43, 53].

59 You see, all this is the Holy Spirit's office

and work. He begins and daily increases holiness upon earth through these two things: the Christian Church and the forgiveness of sin. But in our death He will accomplish it altogether in an instant [1 Corinthians 15:52] and will forever preserve us therein by the last two parts [of the Creed].

But the term "resurrection of the flesh" used 60
here does not agree with good German wording. For when we Germans hear the word *flesh* [Fleisch], we think of nothing more than a butcher block. But in good German wording we would say "resurrection of the body." However, it is not a big issue, as long as we understand the words right.

Now this is the article of the Creed that must 61
always be and remain in use. For we have already received creation. Redemption, too, is finished. But the Holy Spirit carries on His work without ceasing to the Last Day. For that purpose He has appointed a congregation upon earth by which He
speaks and does everything. For He has not yet 62
brought together all His Christian Church [*Christenheit*] [John 10:16] or granted all forgiveness. Therefore, we believe in Him who daily brings us into the fellowship of this Christian Church through the Word. Through the same Word and

the forgiveness of sins He bestows, increases, and strengthens faith. So when He has done it all, and we abide in this and die to the world and to all evil, He may finally make us perfectly and forever holy. Even now we expect this in faith through the Word.

63 See, here you have the entire divine essence, will, and work shown most completely in quite short and yet rich words. In these words all our wisdom stands, which surpasses and exceeds the wisdom, mind, and reason of all people [1 Corinthians 1:18–25]. The whole world with all diligence has struggled to figure out what God is, what He has in mind and does. Yet the world has never been able to grasp ‹the knowledge and understanding of› any of these things. But here we have everything in
64 richest measure. For here in all three articles God has revealed Himself and opened the deepest abyss of His fatherly heart and His pure, inexpressible love [Ephesians 3:18–19]. He has created us for this very reason, that He might redeem and sanctify us. In addition to giving and imparting to us everything in heaven and upon earth, He has even given to us His Son and the Holy Spirit, who brings
65 us to Himself [Romans 8:14, 32]. For (as explained above) we could never grasp the knowledge of the Father's grace and favor except through the

Lord Christ. Jesus is a mirror of the fatherly heart [John 14:9; Colossians 1:15; Hebrews 1:3], outside of whom we see nothing but an angry and terrible Judge. But we couldn't know anything about Christ either, unless it had been revealed by the Holy Spirit [1 Corinthians 2:12].

These articles of the Creed, therefore, divide 66 and separate us Christians from all other people on earth. Even if [or: Even if we were to concede that]* all people outside Christianity—whether heathen, Turks, Jews, or false Christians and hypocrites—believe in and worship only one true God, they still do not know what His mind toward them is and cannot expect any love or blessing from Him. Therefore, they abide in eternal wrath and damnation. For they do not have the Lord Christ, and, besides, are not illumined and favored by any gifts of the Holy Spirit [1 Corinthians 2:9–16; Hebrews 6:4–6].

From this you see that the Creed is a doctrine 67 quite different from the Ten Commandments. For the Commandments teach what we ought to do. But the Creed tells what God does for us and gives to us. Furthermore, apart from this, the Ten Commandments are written in all people's hearts

* See *One True God: Understanding Large Catechism II 66* (St. Louis: Concordia Publishing House, 2006).

[Romans 2:15]. However, no human wisdom can
understand the Creed. It must be taught by the
68 Holy Spirit alone [1 Corinthians 2:12]. The teaching ‹of the Commandments›, therefore, makes no
Christian. For God's wrath and displeasure abide
upon us still, because we cannot keep what God
demands of us. But the Creed brings pure grace
69 and makes us godly and acceptable to God. For
by this knowledge we have love and delight in
all God's commandments [Romans 7:22]. Here
we see that God gives Himself to us completely.
He gives all that He has and is able to do in order
to aid and direct us in keeping the Ten Commandments. The Father gives all creatures. The
Son gives His entire work. And the Holy Spirit
bestows all His gifts.

70 Let this be enough about the Creed to lay a foundation for the simple, so that they may not be burdened. Then, if they understand the substance of it, they themselves may afterward strive to gain more, refer to these parts whatever they learn in the Scriptures, and may ever grow and increase in richer understanding [Ephesians 4:14–15; 2 Peter 3:14]. For as long as we live here, we shall daily have enough to do to preach and to learn this.

CHRIST TEACHES HIS DISCIPLES TO PRAY;
FROM 1530 LARGE CATECHISM

PART 3

PRAYER

THE LORD'S PRAYER

1 We have now heard what we must do and believe, in what things the best and happiest life consists. Now follows the third part, how we ought to
2 pray. For we are in a situation where no person can perfectly keep the Ten Commandments, even though he has begun to believe. The devil with all his power, together with the world and our own flesh, resists our efforts. Therefore, nothing is more necessary than that we should continually turn towards God's ear, call upon Him, and pray to Him. We must pray that He would give, preserve, and increase faith in us and the fulfillment of the Ten Commandments [2 Thessalonians 1:3]. We pray that He would remove everything that is in our way and that opposes us in these matters.
3 So that we might know what and how to pray, our Lord Christ has Himself taught us both the way and the words [Luke 11:1–4], as we shall see.

4 But before we explain the Lord's Prayer part by part, it is most necessary first to encourage and stir people to prayer, as Christ and the apostles

also have done [Matthew 6:5–15]. And the first 5
thing to know is that it is our duty to pray because of God's commandment. For that's what we
heard in the Second Commandment, "You shall
not take the name of the LORD your God in vain"
[Exodus 20:7]. We are required to praise that holy
name and call upon it in every need, or to pray.
To call upon God's name is nothing other than to
pray [e.g., 1 Kings 18:24]. Prayer is just as strictly 6
and seriously commanded as all other commandments: to have no other God, not to kill, not to
steal, and so on. Let no one think that it makes
no difference whether he prays or not. Common
people think this, who grope in such delusion and
ask, "Why should I pray? Who knows whether
God heeds or will hear my prayer? If I do not
pray, someone else will." And so they fall into the
habit of never praying. They build a false argument, as though we taught that there is no duty
or need for prayer, because we reject false and
hypocritical prayers [Matthew 6:5].

But it is certainly true that the prayers that 7
have been offered up till now, when men were
babbling and bawling in the churches [Matthew
6:7], were not prayers. Such outward matters of
prayer, when they are properly done, may be a
good exercise for young children, scholars, and

simple persons. They may be called singing or
8 reading, but not really praying. But praying, as
the Second Commandment teaches, is to call
upon God in every need. He requires this of us
and has not left it to our choice. But it is our
duty and obligation to pray, if we would be
Christians, just as it is our duty and obligation
to obey our parents and the government. For by
calling upon God's name and praying, His name
is honored and used well. This you must note
above all things, so that you may silence and reject thoughts that would keep and deter us from
9 prayer. It would be useless for a son to say to his
father, "What good does my obedience do me?
I will go and do what I can. It makes no difference." But there stands the commandment, "You
shall and must obey." So here prayer is not left
to my will to do it or leave it undone, but it shall
and must be offered at the risk of God's wrath
and displeasure.

10 ‹This point is to be understood and noted before everything else. Then by this point we may silence and cast away the thoughts that would keep
and deter us from praying, as though it does not
matter if we do not pray, or as though prayer was
commanded for those who are holier and in better
favor with God than we are. Indeed, the human

heart is by nature so hopeless that it always flees from God and imagines that He does not wish or desire our prayer, because we are sinners and have earned nothing but wrath [Romans 4:15]. Against 11
such thoughts (I say), we should remember this commandment and turn to God, so that we may not stir up His anger more by such disobedience. For by this commandment God lets us plainly understand that He will not cast us away from Him or chase us away [Romans 11:1]. This is true even though we are sinners. But instead He draws us to Himself [John 6:44], so that we might humble ourselves before Him [1 Peter 5:6], bewail this misery and plight of ours, and pray for grace and help [Psalm 69:13]. Therefore, we read in the Scriptures that He is also angry with those who were punished for their sin, because they did not return to Him and by their prayers turn away His wrath and seek His grace [Isaiah 55:7]›.

Now, from the fact that prayer is so solemnly 12
commanded, you are to conclude and think that no one should in any way despise his prayer. Instead, he should count on prayer. He should 13
always turn to an illustration from the other commandments. A child should in no way despise his obedience to father and mother, but should always think, "This work is a work of obedience.

What I do I do for no other reason than that I may walk in the obedience and commandment of God. On this obedience I can settle and stand firm, and I can value it as a great thing, not because of my worthiness, but because of the commandment." So here also, we should think about the words we pray and the things we pray for as things demanded by God and done in obedience to Him. We should think, "On my account this prayer would amount to nothing. But it shall succeed, because God has commanded it." Therefore, everybody—no matter what he has to say in prayer—should always come before God in obedience to this commandment.

14 We pray, therefore, and encourage everyone
most diligently to take this counsel to heart and
by no means to despise our prayer. For up to
now it has been taught in the devil's name that
no one should think about these things. People
thought it was enough to have done the act of
praying, whether God would hear it or not. But
that is staking prayer on a risk and murmuring
15 it at a venture; therefore, it is a lost prayer. For
we let thoughts like these lead us astray and stop
us: "I am not holy or worthy enough. If I were
as godly and holy as St. Peter or St. Paul, then I
would pray." But put such thoughts far away. For
the same commandment that applied to St. Paul

applies also to me. The Second Commandment is given as much on my account as on his account, so that Paul can boast about no better or holier commandment.

You should say, "My prayer is as precious, 16
holy, and pleasing to God as that of St. Paul or of the most holy saints. This is the reason: I will gladly grant that Paul is personally more holy, but that's not because of the commandment. God does not consider prayer because of the person, but because of His Word and obedience to it. For I rest my prayer on the same commandment on which all the saints rest their prayer. Furthermore, I pray for the same thing that they all pray for and always have prayed. Besides, I have just as great a need of what I pray for as those great saints; no, even a greater one than they."

Let this be the first and most important point, 17
that all our prayers must be based and rest upon obedience to God, regardless of who we are, whether we are sinners or saints, worthy or unworthy. We must know that God will not have 18
our prayer treated as a joke. But He will be angry and punish all who do not pray, just as surely as He punishes all other disobedience. Furthermore, He will not allow our prayers to be in vain or lost. For if He did not intend to answer your prayer, He

would not ask you to pray and add such a severe commandment to it.

19 In the second place, we should be more encouraged and moved to pray because God has also added a promise and declared that it shall surely be done for us as we pray. He says in Psalm 50:15, "Call upon Me in the day of trouble; I will deliver you." And Christ says in the Gospel of St. Matthew, "Ask, and it will be given to you; . . . for
20 everyone who asks receives" (7:7–8). Such promises certainly ought to encourage and kindle our hearts to pray with pleasure and delight. For He testifies with His own Word that our prayer is heartily pleasing to Him. Furthermore, it shall certainly be heard and granted, in order that we may not despise it or think lightly of it and pray based on chance.

21 You can raise this point with Him and say, "Here I come, dear Father, and pray, not because of my own purpose or because of my own worthiness. But I pray because of Your commandment and promise, which cannot fail or deceive me." Whoever, therefore, does not believe this promise must note again that he outrages God like a person who thoroughly dishonors Him and accuses Him of falsehood.

Besides this, we should be moved and drawn to 22
prayer. For in addition to this commandment and
promise, God expects us and He Himself arranges
the words and form of prayer for us. He places
them on our lips for how and what we should pray
[Psalm 51:15], so that we may see how heartily He
pities us in our distress [Psalm 4:1], and we may
never doubt that such prayer is pleasing to Him
and shall certainly be answered. This ‹the Lord's 23
Prayer› is a great advantage indeed over all other
prayers that we might compose ourselves. For in
our own prayers the conscience would ever be in
doubt and say, "I have prayed, but who knows if it
pleases Him or whether I have hit upon the right
proportions and form?" Therefore, there is no nobler prayer to be found upon earth than the Lord's Prayer. We pray it daily [Matthew 6:11], because it has this excellent testimony, that God loves to hear it. We ought not to surrender this for all the riches of the world.

The Lord's Prayer has also been prescribed 24
so that we should see and consider the distress that ought to drive and compel us to pray without ceasing [1 Thessalonians 5:17]. For whoever would pray must have something to present, state, and name, which he desires. If he does not, it cannot be called a prayer.

25 We have rightly rejected the prayers of monks and priests, who howl and growl day and night like fiends. But none of them think of praying for a hair's breadth of anything. If we would assemble all the churches, together with all churchmen, they would be bound to confess that they have never from the heart prayed for even a drop of wine. For none of them has ever intended to pray from obedience to God and faith in His promise. No one has thought about any need. But when they had done their best they thought no further than this: To do a good work, by which they might repay God. They were unwilling to take anything from Him, but wished only to give Him something.

26 But where there is to be a true prayer, there must be seriousness. People must feel their distress, and such distress presses them and compels them to call and cry out. Then prayer will be made willingly, as it ought to be. People will need no teaching about how to prepare for it and to reach
27 the proper devotion. But the distress that ought to concern us most (both for ourselves and everyone), you will find abundantly set forth in the Lord's Prayer. Therefore, this prayer also serves as a reminder, so that we meditate on it and lay it to heart and do not fail to pray. For we all have

enough things that we lack. The great problem is that we do not feel or recognize this. Therefore, God also requires that you weep and ask for such needs and wants, not because He does not know about them [Matthew 6:8], but so that you may kindle your heart to stronger and greater desires and make wide and open your cloak to receive much [Psalm 10:17].

Every one of us should form the daily habit 28
from his youth of praying for all his needs. He should pray whenever he notices anything affecting his interests or that of other people among whom he may live. He should pray for preachers, the government, neighbors, household servants, and always (as we have said) to hold up to God His commandment and promise, knowing that
He will not have them disregarded. This I say 29
because I would like to see these things brought home again to the people so that they might learn to pray truly and not go about coldly and indifferently. They become daily more unfit for prayer because of indifference. That is just what the devil desires, and for which he works with all his powers. He is well aware what damage and harm it does him when prayer is done properly.

We need to know this: all our shelter and 30
protection rest in prayer alone. For we are far too

weak to deal with the devil and all his power and followers who set themselves against us. They might easily crush us under their feet. Therefore, we must consider and take up those weapons with which Christians must be armed in order to stand against the devil [2 Corinthians 10:4; Ephe-
31 sians 6:11]. For what do you imagine has done such great things up till now? What has stopped or quelled the counsels, purposes, murder, and riot of our enemies, by which the devil thought he would crush us, together with the Gospel? It was the prayer of a few godly people standing in the middle like an iron wall for our side. Otherwise they would have witnessed a far different tragedy. They would have seen how the devil would have destroyed all Germany in its own blood. But now our enemies may confidently ridicule prayer and make a mockery of it. However, we shall still be a match both for them and the devil by prayer alone, if we only persevere diligently and do not
32 become slack. For whenever a godly Christian prays, "Dear Father, let Your will be done" [see Matthew 6:10], God speaks from on high and says, "Yes, dear child, it shall be so, in spite of the devil and all the world."

33 Let this be said as encouragement, so that people may learn, first of all, to value prayer as

something great and precious and to make a proper distinction between babbling and praying for
something. For we by no means reject prayer. We
reject the bare, useless howling and murmuring,
as Christ Himself also rejects and prohibits long
idle talk [Matthew 6:7]. Now we shall most briefly 34
and clearly explain the Lord's Prayer. Here there is
included in seven successive articles, or petitions,
every need that never ceases to apply to us. Each
is so great that it ought to drive us to keep praying
the Lord's Prayer all our lives.

THE FIRST PETITION

Hallowed be Thy name. 35

This is, indeed, somewhat difficult, and not expressed in good German. For in our mother tongue we would say, "Heavenly Father, help us in every way so that Your name may be holy." 36

"But what does it mean to pray that His name may be holy? Is it not holy already?" 37

Answer, "Yes, it is always holy in its nature, but in our use it is not holy." For God's name was given to us when we became Christians and were baptized [Matthew 28:19]. So we are called God's children and have the Sacraments, by which He connects us with Himself so that everything that belongs to God must serve for our use [Romans 8:16–17].

38 Now, here is a great need that we ought to be most concerned about. This name should have its proper honor; it should be valued holy and grand as the greatest treasure and holy thing [*Heiligtum*; relic] that we have. As godly children we should pray that God's name, which is already holy in heaven, may also be and remain holy with us upon earth and in all the world.

39 "But how does it become holy among us?"

Answer, as plainly as it can be said: "When both our doctrine and life are godly and Christian." Since we call God our Father in this prayer, it is our duty always to act and behave ourselves as godly children, that He may not receive shame, but honor and praise from us.

40 Now, God's name is profaned by us either through our words or in our works. (For whatever we do upon the earth must be either words
41 or works, speech or act.) In the first place, then, God's name is profaned when people preach, teach, and say in God's name what is false and misleading. They use His name like an ornament and attract a market for falsehood. That is,

indeed, the greatest way to profane and dishonor
the divine name. Furthermore, men, by swear- 42
ing, cursing, conjuring, and other such actions,
grossly abuse the holy name as a cloak for their
shame [1 Peter 2:16]. In the second place, God's 43
name is profaned by an openly wicked life and
works, when those who are called Christians and
God's people are adulterers, drunkards, misers,
enviers, and slanderers [1 Corinthians 5:11]. Here
again God's name must come to shame and be
profaned because of us. It is a shame and disgrace 44
for a flesh-and-blood father to have a bad, perverse child that opposes him in words and deeds. Because of that child the father suffers contempt and reproach. In the same way also, it brings dishonor upon God if we are called by His name and have all kinds of goods from Him, yet we teach, speak, and live in any other way than as godly and heavenly children. People would say about us that we must not be God's children, but the devil's children [1 John 2:29].

So you see that in this petition we pray for 45
exactly what God demands in the Second Commandment. We pray that His name not be taken in vain to swear, curse, lie, deceive, and so on, but be used well for God's praise and honor. For whoever uses God's name for any sort of wrong

profanes and desecrates this holy name. This is how it used to be when a Church was considered desecrated, when a murder or any other crime had been committed in it. Or a monstrance or relic was desecrated—as though they were holy in themselves—when they became unholy by
46 misuse. So this point is easy and clear if only the language is understood: to hallow means the same as to praise, magnify, and honor both in word and deed.

47 Here, now, learn what great need there is for such prayer. Because we see how full the world is of sects and false teachers, who all wear the holy name as a cover and sham for their doctrines of devils [1 Timothy 4:1], we should by all means pray without ceasing [1 Thessalonians 5:17] and cry out and call upon God against all people who preach and believe falsely. We should pray against whatever opposes and persecutes our Gospel and pure doctrine and would suppress it, as do the bishops, tyrants, enthusiasts, and such [2 Thessalonians 2:3–4]. Likewise, we should pray for ourselves who have God's Word but are not thankful for it, nor live like we ought according to the Word.
48 If you pray for this with your heart, you can be sure that it pleases God. For He will not hear anything more dear to Him than that His honor and

praise is exalted above everything else and that His Word is taught in its purity and is considered precious and dear.

THE SECOND PETITION

Thy kingdom come.

In the First Petition we prayed about God's 49
honor and name. We prayed that He would prevent the world from adorning its lies and wickedness with God's name, but that He would cause
His name to be valued as great and holy both in
doctrine and life, so that He may be praised and
magnified in us. Here we pray that His kingdom
also may come. But just as God's name is holy in 50
itself, and we still pray that it be holy among us,
so also His kingdom comes of itself, without our
prayer. Yet we still pray that it may come to us,
that is, triumph among us and with us, so that we
may be a part of those people among whom His
name is hallowed and His kingdom prospers.

"But what is God's kingdom?" 51

Answer, "Nothing other than what we learned in the Creed: God sent His Son, Jesus Christ, our Lord, into the world to redeem and deliver us from the devil's power [1 John 3:8]. He sent Him to bring us to Himself and to govern us as a King of righteousness, life, and salvation against sin, death, and an evil conscience. For this reason He has also given His Holy Spirit, who is to bring these things home to us by His holy Word and to illumine and strengthen us in the faith by His power."

52 We pray here in the first place that this may happen with us. We pray that His name may be so praised through God's holy Word and a Christian life that we who have accepted it may abide and daily grow in it, and that it may gain approval and acceptance among other people. We pray that it may go forth with power throughout the world [2 Thessalonians 3:1]. We pray that many may find entrance into the kingdom of grace [John 3:5], be made partakers of redemption [Colossians 1:12–14], and be led to it by the Holy Spirit [Romans 8:14], so that we may all together remain forever in the one kingdom now begun.

53 For the coming of God's kingdom to us happens in two ways: (a) here in time through the Word and faith [Matthew 13]; and (b) in eternity forever through revelation [Luke 19:11; 1 Peter 1:4–5]. Now we pray for both these things. We pray that the kingdom may come to those who

are not yet in it, and, by daily growth that it may come to us who have received it, both now and hereafter in eternal life. All this is nothing other 54
than saying, "Dear Father, we pray, give us first Your Word, so that the Gospel may be preached properly throughout the world. Second, may the Gospel be received in faith and work and live in us, so that through the Word and the Holy Spirit's power [Romans 15:18–19], Your kingdom may triumph among us. And we pray that the devil's kingdom be put down [Luke 11:17–20], so that he may have no right or power over us [Luke 10:17–19; Colossians 1], until at last his power may be utterly destroyed. So sin, death, and hell shall be exterminated [Revelation 20:13–14]. Then we may live forever in perfect righteousness and blessedness" [Ephesians 4:12–13].

From this you see that we do not pray here 55
for a crust of bread or a temporal, perishable good. Instead, we pray for an eternal inestimable treasure and everything that God Himself possesses. This is far too great for any human heart to think about desiring, if God had not Himself commanded us to pray for the same. But be- 56
cause He is God, He also claims the honor of giving much more and more abundantly than anyone can understand [Ephesians 3:20]. He is

like an eternal, unfailing fountain. The more it pours forth and overflows, the more it continues to give. God desires nothing more seriously from us than that we ask Him for much and great things. In fact, He is angry if we do not ask and pray confidently [Hebrews 4:16].

57 It's like a time when the richest and most mighty emperor would tell a poor beggar to ask whatever he might desire. The emperor was ready to give great royal presents. But the fool would only beg for a dish of gruel. That man would rightly be considered a rogue and a scoundrel, who treated the command of his Imperial Majesty like a joke and a game and was not worthy of coming into his presence. In the same way, it is a great shame and dishonor to God if we—to whom He offers and pledges so many inexpressible treasures—despise the treasures or do not have the confidence to receive them, but hardly dare to pray for a piece of bread.

58 All this is the fault of shameful unbelief that does not even look to God for enough decent food to satisfy the stomach. How much less does such unbelief expect to receive eternal treasures from God without doubt? Therefore, we must strengthen ourselves against such doubt and let this be our first prayer. Then, indeed, we shall

have everything else in abundance, as Christ teaches, "Seek first the kingdom of God and His righteousness, and all these things will be added to you" [Matthew 6:33]. For how could He allow us to suffer lack and to be desperate for temporal things when He promises to give us what is eternal and never perishes [1 Peter 1:4]?

THE THIRD PETITION

Thy will be done on earth as it is in heaven. 59

So far we have prayed that God's name be hon- 60
ored by us and that His kingdom triumph among
us. In these two points is summed up all that deals
with God's honor and our salvation. We receive
God as our own and all His riches. But now arises
a need that is just as great: we must firmly keep
God's honor and our salvation, and not allow ourselves to be torn from them. In a good govern- 61
ment it is not only necessary that there be those
who build and govern well. It is also necessary
to have those who defend, offer protection, and
maintain it firmly. So in God's kingdom, although
we have prayed for the greatest need—for the
Gospel, faith, and the Holy Spirit, that He may
govern us and redeem us from the devil's power—
we must also pray that God's will be done. For

there will be strange events if we are to abide in God's will. We shall have to suffer many thrusts and blows on that account from everything that seeks to oppose and prevent the fulfillment of the first two petitions.

62 No one can believe how the devil opposes and resists these prayers. He cannot allow anyone to teach or to believe rightly. It hurts him beyond measure to have his lies and abominations exposed, which have been honored under the most fancy, sham uses of the divine name. It hurts him when he himself is disgraced, is driven out of the heart, and has to let a breach be made in his kingdom. Therefore, he chafes and rages as a fierce enemy with all his power and might. He marshals all his subjects and, in addition, enlists
63 the world and our own flesh as his allies. For our flesh is in itself lazy and inclined to evil [Romans 7:18], even though we have accepted and believe God's Word. The world, however, is perverse and wicked. So he provokes the world against us, fans and stirs the fire, so that he may hinder and drive us back, cause us to fall, and again bring us under his power [2 Corinthians 2:11; 1 Timothy 3:6–7].
64 Such is all his will, mind, and thought. He strives for this day and night and never rests a moment. He uses all arts, wiles, ways, and means that he can invent.

If we would be Christians, therefore, we must 65
surely expect and count on having the devil with all his angels and the world as our enemies [Matthew 25:41; Revelation 12:9]. They will bring every possible misfortune and grief upon us. For where God's Word is preached, accepted, or believed and produces fruit, there the holy cross cannot be missing [Acts 14:22]. And let no one think that he shall have peace [Matthew 10:34]. He must risk whatever he has upon earth—possessions, honor, house and estate, wife and children, body and life. Now, this hurts our flesh 66
and the old Adam [Ephesians 4:22]. The test is to be steadfast and to suffer with patience [James 5:7–8] in whatever way we are assaulted, and to let go whatever is taken from us [1 Peter 2:20–21].

So there is just as great a need, as in all the 67
other petitions, that we pray without ceasing, "Dear Father, Your will be done, not the devil's will or our enemies' or anything that would persecute and suppress Your holy Word or hinder Your kingdom. Grant that we may bear with patience and overcome whatever is to be endured because of Your Word and kingdom, so that our poor flesh may not yield or fall away because of weakness or sluggishness."

68 Look, we have in these three petitions, in the simplest way, the needs that relate to God Himself. Yet they are all for our sakes. Whatever we pray concerns us alone. As we have said before, we pray that what must be done without us anyway may also be done in us. As His name must be hallowed and His kingdom come whether we pray or not, so also His will must be done and succeed. This is true even though the devil with all his followers raise a great riot, are angry and rage against it, and try to exterminate the Gospel completely. But for our own sakes we must pray that, even against their fury, His will be done without hindrance among us also. We pray so that they may not be able to accomplish anything and that we may remain firm against all violence and persecution and submit to God's will.

69 Such prayer, then, is to be our protection and defense now. It is to repel and put down all that the devil, pope, bishops, tyrants, and heretics can do against our Gospel. Let them all rage and attempt their utmost and deliberate and resolve how they may suppress and exterminate us, so that their will and counsel may prevail. Over and against this one or two Christians with this petition alone shall be our wall [Ezekiel 22:30], against which they shall run and dash themselves

to pieces. We have this comfort and confidence: 70
the devil's will and purpose and all our enemies shall and must fail and come to nothing, no matter how proud, secure, and powerful they know themselves to be. For if their will were not broken and hindered, God's kingdom could not remain on earth nor His name be hallowed.

THE FOURTH PETITION

Give us this day our daily bread. 71

Here, now, we consider the poor breadbasket, 72
the necessities of our body and of the temporal life. It is a brief and simple word, but it has a very wide scope. For when you mention and pray for daily bread, you pray for everything that is necessary in order to have and enjoy daily bread. On the other hand, you also pray against everything that interferes with it. Therefore, you must open wide and extend your thoughts not only to the oven or the flour bin, but also to the distant field and the entire land, which bears and brings to us daily bread and every sort of nourishment. For if God did not cause food to grow and He did not bless and preserve it in the field, we could never take bread from the oven or have any to set upon the table.

73 To sum things up, this petition includes everything that belongs to our entire life in the world, for we need daily bread because of life alone. It is not only necessary for our life that our body have food and clothes and other necessaries. It is also necessary that we spend our days in peace and quiet among the people with whom we live and have dealings in daily business and conversation and all sorts of doings [1 Thessalonians 4:11; 2 Thessalonians 3:12; 1 Timothy 2:2]. In short, this petition applies both to the household and also to the neighborly or civil relationship and government. Where these two things are hindered so that they do not prosper as they should, the necessaries of life also are hindered. Ultimately, life cannot be maintained.
74 There is, indeed, the greatest need to pray for earthly authority and government. By them, most of all, God preserves for us our daily bread and all the comforts of this life. Though we have received from God all good things in abundance, we are not able to keep any of them or use them in security and happiness if He did not give us a permanent and peaceful government. For where there are dissension, strife, and war, there the daily bread is already taken away or is at least hindered.

It would be very proper to place on the coat of 75
arms of every pious prince a loaf of bread instead of a lion or a wreath of herbs. Or one could impress it on money. This would remind both princes and their subjects that by their office we have protection and peace. Without them, we could not eat and keep our daily bread. Therefore, princes are also worthy of all honor. We should give to them for their office what we ought and can, as to people through whom we enjoy what we have in peace and quietness. Otherwise we would not keep a farthing. In addition, we should also pray for them [1 Timothy 2:1–2] that through them God may bestow on us more blessings and goods.

Let this be a very brief explanation and sketch, 76
showing how far this petition extends through all conditions on earth. On this topic anyone might indeed make a long prayer. With many words one could list all the things that are included, like when we ask God to give us food and drink, clothing, house and home, and health of body. Or when we ask that He cause the grain and fruit of the field to grow and mature well. Furthermore, we ask that He help us at home with good housekeeping and that He give and preserve for us a godly wife, children, and servants. We ask that He cause our work, trade, or whatever we are engaged in to

prosper and succeed, favor us with faithful neighbors and good friends, and other such things.
77 Likewise, we ask that He give wisdom, strength, and success to emperors, kings, and all estates, and especially to the rulers of our country and to all counselors, magistrates, and officers. Then they may govern well and vanquish the Turks and all enemies. We ask that He give to subjects and the common people obedience, peace, and harmony
78 in their life with one another. On the other hand, we ask that He would preserve us from all sorts of disaster to body and livelihood, like lightning, hail, fire, flood, poison, plague, cattle disease, war and bloodshed, famine, destructive beasts, wicked
79 men, and so forth. It is well to impress all this upon the common people [Deuteronomy 6:7]: these things come from God and must be prayed for by us.

80 But this petition is especially directed also against our chief enemy, the devil. For all his thought and desire is to deprive us of all that we have from God or to hinder it. He is not satisfied to obstruct and destroy spiritual government by leading souls astray with his lies and bringing them under his power. He also prevents and hinders the stability of all government and honorable, peaceable relations on earth. There

he causes so much contention, murder, treason, and war. He also causes lightning and hail to destroy grain and cattle, to poison the air, and
so on. In short, he is sorry if anyone has a morsel 81
of bread from God and eats it in peace. If it were in his power and our prayer (next to God) did not prevent him, we would not keep a straw in the field, a farthing in the house, yes, not even our life for an hour. This is especially true of those who have God's Word and would like to be Christians.

You see, in this way, God wishes to show us 82
how He cares for us in all our need and faithfully
provides also for our earthly support. He abun- 83
dantly grants and preserves these things, even for the wicked and rogues [Matthew 5:45]. Yet, He wishes that we pray for these goods in order that we may recognize that we receive them from His hand and may feel His fatherly goodness toward us in them [Psalm 104:28; 145:16]. For when He withdraws His hand, nothing can prosper or be maintained in the end. Indeed, we daily see this
and experience it. How much trouble there is 84
now in the world only on account of bad coins, daily oppression, raising of prices in common trade, and bargaining and labor by those who greedily oppress the poor and deprive them of

their daily bread! This we must suffer indeed. But let such people take care so that they do not lose the benefits of common intercession. Let them beware lest this petition in the Lord's Prayer speak against them.

THE FIFTH PETITION

85 **And forgive us our trespasses as we forgive those who trespass against us.**

86 This part now applies to our poor miserable life. Although we have and believe God's Word, do and submit to His will, and are supported by His gifts and blessings, our life is still not sinless. We still stumble daily and transgress because we live in the world among people. They do us much harm and give us reasons for impatience, anger,
87 revenge, and such. Besides, we have the devil at our back. He attacks us from every side and fights—as we have heard—against all the previous petitions. So it is not possible to stand firm at all times in such a constant conflict.

88 There is here again great need for us to call upon God and to pray, "Dear Father, forgive us our trespasses." It is not as though He did not forgive sin without and even before our prayer. (He has given us the Gospel, in which is pure

forgiveness before we prayed or ever thought
about it [Romans 5:8].) But the purpose of this
prayer is that we may recognize and receive such
forgiveness. The flesh in which we daily live is of 89
such a nature that it neither trusts nor believes
God [Romans 7:14–18]. It is ever active in evil
lusts and devices, so that we sin daily in word
and deed [Genesis 6:5], by what we do and fail
to do [James 2:15–16]. By this the conscience is
thrown into unrest, so that it is afraid of God's
wrath and displeasure. So it loses the comfort and
confidence derived from the Gospel. Therefore, it
is always necessary that we run here and receive
consolation to comfort the conscience again.

But this should serve God's purpose of break- 90
ing our pride and keeping us humble. God has
reserved this right for Himself: if anyone wants
to boast of his godliness and despise others, that
person is to think about himself and place this
prayer before his eyes. He will find that he is no
better than others [Romans 12:3] and that in
God's presence all must tuck their tails and be
glad that they can gain forgiveness. Let no one 91
think that as long as he lives here he can reach
such a position that he will not need such forgiveness [1 John 1:8]. In short, if God does not forgive
without stopping, we are lost.

92 It is, therefore, the intent of this petition that God would not regard our sins and hold up to us what we daily deserve. But we pray that He would deal graciously with us and forgive, as He has promised, and so grant us a joyful and confident conscience to stand before Him in prayer [Hebrews 10:22]. For where the heart is not in a right relationship with God, or cannot take such confidence, it will not dare to pray anymore. Such a confident and joyful heart can spring from nothing else than the certain knowledge of the forgiveness of sin [Psalm 32:1–2; Romans 4:7–8].

93 There is here attached a necessary, yet comforting addition: "As we forgive." He has promised that we shall be sure that everything is forgiv-
en and pardoned, in the way that we also forgive
94 our neighbor. Just as we daily sin much against
God, and yet He forgives everything through
grace, so we, too, must ever forgive our neighbor
who does us injury, violence, and wrong, shows
95 malice toward us, and so on. If, therefore, you do
not forgive, then do not think that God forgives
you [Matthew 18:23–25]. But if you forgive, you
have this comfort and assurance, that you are
96 forgiven in heaven. This is not because of your
forgiving. For God forgives freely and without
condition, out of pure grace, because He has so

promised, as the Gospel teaches. But God says this in order that He may establish forgiveness as our confirmation and assurance, as a sign alongside of the promise, which agrees with this prayer in Luke 6:37, "Forgive, and you will be forgiven." Therefore, Christ also repeats it soon after the Lord's Prayer, and says in Matthew 6:14, "For if you forgive others their trespasses, your heavenly Father will also forgive you," and so on.

This sign is therefore attached to this petition. 97
When we pray, we remember the promise and think, "Dear Father, for this reason I come and pray for You to forgive me, not so that I can make satisfaction or can merit anything by my works. I pray because You have promised and attached the seal to this prayer that I should be as sure about it as though I had Absolution pronounced by You
Yourself." For Baptism and the Lord's Supper— 98
appointed as outward signs—work as seals [Ephesians 1:13]. In the same way also, this sign can serve to confirm our consciences and cause them to rejoice. It is especially given for this purpose, so that we may use and practice forgiveness every hour, as a thing that we have with us at all times.

THE SIXTH PETITION

99 **And lead us not into temptation.**

100 We have now heard enough about what toil and labor is needed to keep all that we pray for and to persevere. This, however, is not done without weakness and stumbling. Although we have received forgiveness and a good conscience and are entirely acquitted, yet our life is of such a nature that we stand today, and tomorrow we fall [Isaiah 40:6–8]. Therefore, even though we are godly now and stand before God with a good conscience, we must pray again that He would not allow us to fall again and yield to trials and temptations.

101 Temptation, however, or (as our Saxons in olden times used to call it) *Bekörunge*, is of three kinds: of the flesh, of the world, and of the devil.
102 For we dwell in the flesh and carry the old Adam about our neck. He exerts himself and encourages us daily to unchastity, laziness, gluttony and drunkenness, greed and deception, to defraud our neighbor and to overcharge him [Galatians 5:19–21; Colossians 3:5–8]. In short, the old Adam encourages us to have all kinds of evil lusts, which cling to us by nature and to which we are moved by the society, the example, and

what we hear and see of other people. They often wound and inflame even an innocent heart.

Next comes the world, which offends us in word and deed. It drives us to anger and impatience. In short, there is nothing but hatred and envy, hostility, violence and wrong, unfaithfulness, vengeance, cursing, railing, slander, pride and haughtiness, with useless finery, honor, fame, and power. No one is willing to be the least. Everyone desires to sit at the head of the group and to be seen before all [Luke 14:7–11]. 103

Then comes the devil, pushing and provoking in all directions. But he especially agitates matters that concern the conscience and spiritual affairs. He leads us to despise and disregard both God's Word and works. He tears us away from faith, hope, and love [1 Corinthians 13:13], and he brings us into misbelief, false security, and stubbornness. Or, on the other hand, he leads us to despair, denial of God, blasphemy, and innumerable other shocking things. These are snares and nets [2 Timothy 2:26], indeed, real fiery darts that are shot like poison into the heart, not by flesh and blood, but by the devil [Ephesians 6:12, 16]. 104

Great and grievous, indeed, are these dangers and temptations, which every Christian must 105 bear. We bear them even though each one were alone by himself. So every hour that we are in this vile life, we are attacked on all sides [2 Corinthians 4:8], chased and hunted down. We are moved to cry out and to pray that God would not allow us to become weary and faint [Isaiah 40:31; Hebrews 12:3] and to fall again into sin, shame, and unbelief. For otherwise it is impossible to overcome even the least temptation.

106 This, then, is what "lead us not into temptation" means. It refers to times when God gives us power and strength to resist the temptation [1 Corinthians 10:13]. However, the temptation is not taken away or removed. While we live in the flesh and have the devil around us, no one can escape his temptation and lures. It can only mean that we must endure trials—indeed, be engulfed in them [2 Timothy 2:3]. But we say this prayer so that we may not fall and be drowned in them.

107 To feel temptation is, therefore, a far different thing from consenting or yielding to it. We must all feel it, although not all in the same way. Some feel it in a greater degree and more severely than others. For example, the young suffer especially from the flesh. Afterward, when they reach middle life and old age, they feel it from the world. But others who are occupied with spiritual

matters, that is, strong Christians, feel it from the
devil. Such feeling, as long as it is against our will 108
and we would rather be rid of it, can harm no one. For if we did not feel it, it could not be called a temptation. But we consent to it when we give it the reins and do not resist or pray against it.

Therefore, we Christians must be armed 109
[Ephesians 6:10–18] and daily expect to be constantly attacked. No one may go on in security and carelessly, as though the devil were far from us. At all times we must expect and block his blows. Though I am now chaste, patient, kind, and in firm faith, the devil will this very hour send such an arrow into my heart that I can scarcely stand. For he is an enemy that never stops or becomes tired. So when one temptation stops, there always arise others and fresh ones.

So there is no help or comfort except to run 110
here, take hold of the Lord's Prayer, and speak to God from the heart like this: "Dear Father, You have asked me to pray. Don't let me fall because of temptations." Then you will see that the temptations must stop and finally confess themselves
conquered. If you try to help yourself by your 111
own thoughts and counsel, you will only make the matter worse and give the devil more space. For he has a serpent's head [Revelation 12:9]. If it

finds an opening into which it can slip, the whole body will follow without stopping. But prayer can prevent him and drive him back.

THE SEVENTH AND LAST PETITION

112 **But deliver us from evil. Amen.**

113 In the Greek text this petition reads, "Deliver or preserve us from the evil one," or "the hateful one." It looks like Jesus was speaking about the devil, like He would summarize every petition in one. So the entire substance of all our prayer is directed against our chief enemy. For it is he who hinders among us everything that we pray for: God's name or honor, God's kingdom and will, our daily bread, a cheerful good conscience, and so forth.

114 Therefore, we finally sum it all up and say,
"Dear Father, grant that we be rid of all these
115 disasters." But there is also included in this petition whatever evil may happen to us under the devil's kingdom: poverty, shame, death, and, in short, all the agonizing misery and heartache of which there is such an unnumbered multitude on the earth. Since the devil is not only a liar, but also a murderer [John 8:44], he constantly seeks

our life. He wreaks his vengeance whenever he can afflict our bodies with misfortune and harm. Therefore, it happens that he often breaks men's necks or drives them to insanity, drowns some, and moves many to commit suicide and to many
other terrible disasters [e.g., Mark 9:17–22]. So 116
there is nothing for us to do upon earth but to pray against this archenemy without stopping. For unless God preserved us, we would not be safe from this enemy even for an hour.

You see again how God wishes for us to pray 117
to Him also for all the things that affect our bodily interests, so that we seek and expect help nowhere
else except in Him. But He has put this matter 118
last. For if we are to be preserved and delivered from all evil, God's name must first be hallowed in us, His kingdom must be with us, and His will must be done. After that He will finally preserve us from sin and shame, and, besides, from everything that may hurt or harm us.

So God has briefly placed before us all the 119
distress that may ever come upon us, so that we might have no excuse whatever for not praying. But all depends upon this, that we learn also to say "Amen." This means that we do not doubt that our prayer is surely heard and that what we pray
shall be done [2 Corinthians 1:20]. This is nothing 120

else than the word of undoubting faith, which does not pray on a dare but knows that God does not lie to him [Titus 1:2]. For He has promised to grant it. Therefore, where there is no such faith, there cannot be true prayer either.

121 It is, therefore, an evil deception on those who pray as though they could not dare from the heart to say "Yes!" and positively conclude that God hears them. Instead, they remain in doubt and say, "How can I be so bold as to boast that God hears my prayer? For I am but a poor sinner," and other such things.

122 The reason for this is, they do not respect God's promise, but they rely on their own work and worthiness, by which they despise God and
123 accuse Him of lying. Therefore, they receive nothing. As St. James says, "But let him ask in faith, with no doubting, for the one who doubts is like a wave of the sea that is driven and tossed by the wind. For that person must not suppose that he will receive anything from the Lord"
124 [1:6–7]. Behold, God attaches such importance to this fact that we can be sure we do not pray in vain, so that we do not despise our prayer in any way.

PART 4
BAPTISM

We have now finished the three chief parts 1
of common Christian doctrine. Besides these we
have yet to speak of our two Sacraments instituted
by Christ. Every Christian also ought to have at
least an ordinary, brief instruction about the
Sacraments, because without them he cannot be
a Christian. Unfortunately, up to now, no instruction about them has been given. But, in the first 2
place, we take up Baptism, by which we are first
received into the Christian Church [John 3:5].
However, in order that Baptism may be easily understood, we will present it in an orderly manner.
We present only what is necessary for us to know.
We will leave to the learned the topic of how
Baptism is to be maintained and defended against
heretics and sects.

In the first place, we must above all things 3
know well the words on which Baptism is founded. Everything refers to these words that must
be said on the subject. The Lord Christ says in
Matthew 28:19:

> Go therefore and make disciples of all na- 4
> tions, baptizing them in the name of the

Father and of the Son and of the Holy Spirit.

Likewise in St. Mark 16:16:

5 Whoever believes and is baptized will be saved, but whoever does not believe will be condemned.

6 In the first place, you must note in these words that here stand God's commandment and institution. Let us not doubt that Baptism is divine. It is not made up or invented by people. For as surely as I can say, "No one has spun the Ten Commandments, the Creed, and the Lord's Prayer out of his head; they are revealed and given by God Himself." So also I can boast that Baptism is no human plaything, but it is instituted by God Himself. Furthermore, Baptism is most solemnly and strictly commanded so that we must be baptized or we cannot be saved. I note this lest anyone regard Baptism as a silly matter, like putting
7 on a new red coat. For it is of the greatest importance that we value Baptism as excellent, glorious, and exalted. We contend and fight for Baptism chiefly because the world is now so full of sects arguing that Baptism is an outward thing and that
8 outward things are of no benefit. But let Baptism be a thoroughly outward thing. Here stand God's Word and command, which institute, establish, and confirm Baptism. What God institutes and

commands cannot be an empty thing. It must be a most precious thing, even though it looked like
it had less value than a straw. Up to now people 9
could consider something great when the pope with his letters and bulls gave away indulgences and confirmed altars and churches, solely because of the letters and seals. So we ought to value Baptism much more highly and more precious, because God has commanded it. Besides, it is done in His name. For these are the words, "Go, baptize." However, do not baptize in your name, but in God's name.

To be baptized in God's name is to be bap- 10
tized not by men, but by God Himself. Therefore, although it is performed by human hands, it is still truly God's own work. From this fact everyone may readily conclude that Baptism is a far higher work than any work performed by a man or a saint. For what work can we do that is greater than God's work?

But here the devil is busy to fool us with false 11
appearances and lead us away from God's work to our own works. For there is a much more splendid show when a Carthusian does many great and difficult works. We all think much more
of the things that we do and merit ourselves. But 12
the Scriptures teach this: Even though we collect

in one pile the works of all the monks, however splendidly they may shine, they would not be as noble and good as if God should pick up a single straw. Why? Because the person is nobler and better. Here, then, we must not judge the person according to the works, but the works according to the person [Matthew 7:16–20], from whom
13 they must get their nobility. But our insane reason will not consider this. Because Baptism does not shine like the works that we do, it is valued as nothing.

14 From this now learn a proper understanding of the subject and how to answer the question of what Baptism is. It is not mere ordinary water, but water comprehended in God's Word and command and sanctified by them [Ephesians 5:26–27]. So it is nothing other than a divine water. Not that the water in itself is nobler than other water, but that God's Word and command are added to it.

15 It is pure wickedness and blasphemy of the devil when our "new spirits" mock Baptism, leaving God's Word and institution out of it. They look at Baptism in no other way than as water that is taken from the well. Then they blather and say, "How does a handful of water help the
16 soul?" Yes, my friend, who does not know that

water is water? (If tearing things apart is what we are after.) But how dare you interfere with God's order? How dare you tear away the most precious treasure with which God has connected and enclosed Baptism, and that He will not allow to be separated? For the kernel in the water is God's Word or command and God's name. His name is a treasure greater and nobler than heaven and earth.

Understand the difference, then. Baptism is 17
quite a different thing from all other water. This is not because of its natural quality but because something more noble is added here. God Himself stakes His honor, His power, and His might on it. Therefore, Baptism is not only natural water, but a divine, heavenly, holy, and blessed water, and whatever other terms we can find to praise it. This is all because of the Word, which is a heavenly, holy Word, which no one can praise enough. For it has, and is able to do, all that God
is and can do [Isaiah 55:10–11]. In this way it also 18
gets its essence as a Sacrament, as St. Augustine also taught, "When the Word is joined to the element or natural substance, it becomes a Sacrament," that is, a holy and divine matter and sign.

We always teach that the Sacraments and all 19
outward things that God ordains and institutes

should not be considered according to the coarse,
outward mask, the way we look at a nutshell. But
we respect them because God's Word is included
20 in them. For we also speak of the parental estate
and of civil government in this way. If we intend
only to recognize that they have noses, eyes, skin,
and hair, flesh and bones, they look like Turks
and heathen. Someone might start up and say,
"Why should I value them more than others?"
Because this commandment is added, "Honor
your father and your mother" [Exodus 20:12]. I
see a different person, adorned and clothed with
God's majesty and glory. The commandment, I
say, is the gold chain about his neck. Yes, that is
the crown upon his head, which shows me how
and why one must honor this flesh and blood.

21 So, and even much more, you must honor Baptism and consider it glorious because of the Word. For God Himself has honored it both by words and deeds. Furthermore, He confirmed it with miracles from heaven. Do you think it was a joke that, when Christ was baptized, the heavens were opened and the Holy Spirit descended visibly, and everything was divine glory and majesty [Luke 3:21–22]?

22 I encourage again that these two—the water and the Word—by no means be separated from

each other and parted. For if the Word is separated from it, the water is the same as the water that the servant cooks with. It may indeed be called a bath-keeper's baptism. But when the Word is added, as God has ordained, it is a Sacrament. It is called Christ's Baptism. Let this be the first part about the holy Sacrament's essence and dignity.

In the second place, since we know now what 23
Baptism is and how it is to be regarded, we must also learn why and for what purpose it is instituted. We must learn what it profits, gives, and works. For this also we cannot find a better resource than Christ's words quoted above, "Whoever believes and is baptized will be saved" [Mark
16:16]. Therefore, state it most simply in this 24
way: the power, work, profit, fruit, and purpose of Baptism is this—to save [1 Peter 3:21]. For no one is baptized in order that he may become a prince, but, as the words say, that he "be saved."
We know that to be saved is nothing other than 25
to be delivered from sin, death, and the devil [Colossians 1:13–14]. It means to enter into Christ's kingdom [John 3:5], and to live with Him forever.

Here you see again how highly and preciously 26
we should value Baptism, because in it we receive such an unspeakable treasure. This also proves that it cannot be ordinary, mere water. For mere

water could not do such a thing. But the Word does it and, as I said above, so does the fact that
27 God's name is included in Baptism. Where God's name is, there must also be life and salvation [Psalm 54:1]. So Baptism may certainly be called a divine, blessed, fruitful, and gracious water. Such power is given to Baptism by the Word that it is a washing of new birth, as St. Paul also calls it in Titus 3:5.

28 Our would-be wise, "new spirits" assert that faith alone saves, and that works and outward things do nothing. We answer, "It is true, indeed, that nothing in us is of any use but faith,
29 as we shall hear still further." But these blind guides are unwilling to see this: faith must have something that it believes, that is, of which it takes hold [2 Timothy 1:13; Titus 1:9] and upon which it stands and rests [1 Corinthians 2:5]. So faith clings to the water and believes that in Baptism, there is pure salvation and life. This is not through the water (as we have stated well enough), but through the fact that it is embodied in God's Word and institution, and that God's name abides in it. Now, if I believe this, what else is it than believing in God as the One who has given and planted His Word [Mark 4:14] into this ordinance and offers to us this outward thing by which we may gain such a treasure?

Now, these "new spirits" are so crazy that they 30
separate faith and the object to which faith clings
and is bound, even if it is something outward.
Yes, it shall and must be something outward, so
that it may be grasped by our senses and understood, and by them be brought into the heart.
For indeed, the entire Gospel is an outward,
verbal preaching [Romans 10:17; 1 Corinthians
1:21]. In short, what God does and works in us
He intends to work through such outward ordinances. Therefore, wherever He speaks—indeed,
no matter what direction or by whatever means
He speaks—faith must look there. It must hold to 31
that object. Now here we have the words "Whoever believes and is baptized will be saved" [Mark
16:16]. What else can these words refer to but
Baptism, that is, to the water included in God's
ordinance? Therefore, it makes sense that whoever rejects Baptism rejects God's Word, faith,
and Christ, who directs us to Baptism and binds
us to Baptism.

In the third place, since we have learned Bap- 32
tism's great benefit and power, let us see further
who is the person that receives what Baptism
gives and profits. This is again most beautifully 33
and clearly expressed in the words "Whoever believes and is baptized will be saved" [Mark 16:16].

That is, faith alone makes the person worthy to
receive profitably the saving, divine water. Since
these blessings are presented here and promised
through the words in and with the water, they
cannot be received in any other way than by be-
34 lieving them with the heart [Romans 10:9]. Without faith it profits nothing, even though Baptism
is in itself a divine overwhelming treasure. Therefore, this single phrase, "Whoever believes," does
so much. It excludes and repels all the works that
we can do, when we suppose that we gain and
merit salvation by our works. For it is determined
that whatever is not faith does nothing or receives
nothing [Hebrews 11:6].

35 But if the "new spirits" say, as they are accustomed, "Still Baptism is itself a work, and you
say works are of no use for salvation. What, then,
becomes of faith?" Answer, "Yes, our works, indeed, do nothing for salvation. Baptism, however,
is not our work, but God's." For, as was stated,
you must completely distinguish Christ's Baptism from a bathkeeper's baptism. God's works
are saving and necessary for salvation. They do
not exclude, but demand, faith. For without faith
36 they could not be grasped. By allowing the water
to be poured upon you, you have not yet received
Baptism in a way that benefits you at all. But it

becomes beneficial to you if you have yourself baptized with this thought: this is according to God's command and ordinance, and besides, it is done in God's name. In this way you may receive the promised salvation in the water. Now, your fist cannot do this, nor your body; but the heart must believe it [Ezekiel 36:25–26; Hebrews 10:22].

So you see plainly that there is no work done 37
here by us, but a treasure, which God gives us and faith grasps [Ephesians 2:8–9]. It is like the benefit of the Lord Jesus Christ upon the cross, which is not a work, but a treasure included in the Word. It is offered to us and received by faith. Therefore, the "new spirits" violate us by shouting against us as though we preach against faith. For we alone insist upon it as being so necessary that without it nothing can be received or enjoyed.

So we have these three parts, which must 38
be known about this Sacrament, especially that God's ordinance is to be held in all honor. The Sacrament alone would be enough, even though it is an entirely outward thing. It is like the commandment "Honor your father and your mother," which refers to bodily flesh and blood. In these words we do not think about the flesh and blood, but God's commandment in which flesh

and blood are included, and on account of which the flesh is called father and mother. So even if we had only these words, "Go and baptize," or such, it would be necessary for us to accept them and
39 do them as God's ordinance. Now there is not only God's commandment and injunction here, but also the promise. Because of this, Baptism is still far more glorious than whatever else God has commanded and ordained. It is, in short, so full of consolation and grace that heaven and earth
40 cannot understand it. But it requires skill to believe this, for the treasure is not lacking, but this is lacking: people who grasp it and hold it firmly.

41 Therefore, every Christian has enough in Baptism to learn and to do all his life. For he has always enough to do by believing firmly what Baptism promises and brings: victory over death and the devil [Romans 6:3–6], forgiveness of sin [Acts 2:38], God's grace [Titus 3:5–6], the entire Christ, and the Holy Spirit with His gifts [1 Cor-
42 inthians 6:11]. In short, Baptism is so far beyond us that if timid nature could realize this, it might
43 well doubt whether it could be true. Think about it. Imagine there was a doctor somewhere who understood the art of saving people from death or, even though they died, could restore them quickly to life so that they would afterward live

forever. Oh, how the world would pour in money like snow and rain. No one could find access to him because of the throng of the rich! But here in Baptism there is freely brought to everyone's door such a treasure and medicine that it utterly destroys death and preserves all people alive.

We must think this way about Baptism and 44
make it profitable for ourselves. So when our sins
and conscience oppress us, we strengthen ourselves and take comfort and say, "Nevertheless, I
am baptized. And if I am baptized, it is promised
to me that I shall be saved and have eternal life,
both in soul and body." For that is the reason 45
why these two things are done in Baptism: the
body—which can grasp nothing but the water—is
sprinkled and, in addition, the Word is spoken
for the soul to grasp. Now, since both, the water 46
and the Word, make one Baptism, therefore,
body and soul must be saved and live forever
[1 Corinthians 15:53]. The soul lives through the
Word, which it believes, but the body lives because it is united with the soul and also holds
on through Baptism as it is able to grasp it. We
have, therefore, no greater jewel in body and soul.
For by Baptism we are made holy and are saved
[1 Corinthians 6:11]. No other kind of life, no
work upon earth, can do this.

Let this be enough about Baptism's nature, blessing, and use, for it fulfills the present purpose.

INFANT BAPTISM

47 Here a question arises by which the devil, through his sects, confuses the world: Infant Baptism. Do children also believe? Are they rightly
48 baptized? Briefly we say about this, let the simple dismiss this question from their minds. Refer it to the learned. But if you wish to answer, answer as follows:

49 The Baptism of infants is pleasing to Christ, as is proved well enough from His own work. For God sanctifies many of those who have been baptized as infants and has given them the Holy Spirit. There are still many people even today in whom we perceive that they have the Holy Spirit both because of their doctrine and life. It is also given to us by God's grace that we can explain the Scriptures and come to the knowledge of Christ, which is impossible without the Holy Spirit
50 [1 Corinthians 12:3]. But if God did not accept the Baptism of infants, He would not give the Holy Spirit nor any of His gifts to any of them. In short, during the long time up to this day, no person on earth could have been a Christian. Now,

God confirms Baptism by the gifts of His Holy Spirit, as is plainly seen in some of the Church Fathers, like St. Bernard, Gerson, John Hus, and others. These people were baptized in infancy, and since the holy Christian Church cannot perish until the end of the world, the sects must acknowledge that such infant Baptism is pleasing to God. For God can never be opposed to Himself or support falsehood and wickedness, or for its promotion impart His grace and Spirit.
51 This is indeed the best and strongest proof for the simpleminded and unlearned. For the sects shall not take from us or overthrow this article: "I believe in . . . the holy Christian Church, the communion of saints."

52 Further, we say that we are not very concerned to know whether the person baptized believes or not. For Baptism does not become invalid on that account.
53 But everything depends on God's Word and command. Now this point is perhaps somewhat difficult. But it rests entirely on what I have said, that Baptism is nothing other than water and God's Word in and with each other [Ephesians 5:26]. That is, when the Word is added to the water, Baptism is valid, even though faith is lacking. For my faith does not make Baptism, but receives it. Now, Baptism does not become invalid even though it

is wrongly received or used. As stated above, it is not bound to our faith, but to the Word.

54 Suppose a Jewish person should come dishonestly today and with evil intent, and we should baptize him in all good faith. We must say that his Baptism is still genuine. For here is the water together with God's Word, even though the person does not receive it as he should. It is like those who go to the Sacrament [Lord's Supper] unworthily yet still receive the true Sacrament, even though they do not believe [1 Corinthians 11:27].

55 So you see that the objection of the sectarians is empty. As we have said, even though infants did not believe (which, however, is not the case), still their Baptism would be valid. We have now shown this. No one should rebaptize infants. Nothing is taken away from the Sacrament even though someone approaches it with evil purpose. So he could not be allowed to take it a second time the self-same hour on account of his abuse, as though he had not received the true Sacrament at first. That would blaspheme and profane the Sacrament in the worst way. How dare we think that God's Word and ordinance should be wrong and invalid because we make a wrong use of it?

56 I say, if you did not believe then, believe now and say this: The Baptism certainly was right. But

I, unfortunately, did not receive it aright. I myself also, and all who are baptized, must say this before God, "I come here in my faith and in that of others. Yet I cannot rest in this, that I believe, and that many people pray for me. But in this I rest, that Baptism is Your Word and command. It is just like when I go to the Sacrament trusting not in my faith, but in Christ's Word. Whether I am strong or weak, I commit that to God. But I know this, that He asks me to go, to eat and to drink, and so on, and He gives me His body and blood [Matthew 26:26–28]. That will not deceive me or prove false to me."

So we do likewise in infant Baptism. We 57
bring the child in the conviction and hope that it believes, and we pray that God may grant it faith [Luke 17:2; Ephesians 2:8]. But we do not baptize it for that reason, but solely because of God's command. Why? Because we know that God does not lie [Titus 1:2]. I and my neighbor and, in short, all people, may err and deceive. But God's Word cannot err.

They are arrogant, clumsy minds that draw 58
together such ideas and conclusions as these, "Where there is not the true faith, there also cannot be true Baptism." That's as if I would conclude, "If I do not believe, then Christ is nothing."

Or "If I am not obedient, then father, mother, and government are nothing." Is that a correct conclusion, that whenever anyone does not do what he ought, the work that he ought to do shall become
59 nothing and of no value? My dear, just invert the argument and rather draw this conclusion: For this very reason Baptism *is* something and *is* right, because it has been wrongly received. For if Baptism was not right and true in itself, it could not be misused or sinned against. The saying is, "Abuse does not destroy the essence, but confirms it." For gold is not the less gold even though a harlot wears it in sin and shame.

60 Therefore, let it be decided that Baptism always remains true and retains its full essence. This is true even though a single person should be baptized, and he, in addition, should not truly believe. For God's ordinance and Word cannot be made
61 inconsistent or be changed by people. But these people, the fanatics, are so blind that they do not see God's Word and command. They think about Baptism and those who administer it just like they think about water in the brook or in pots, or like any common person. Because they do not see faith or obedience in infants, they conclude that
62 infant Baptisms are to be considered invalid. Here lurks a concealed rebellious devil, who would like

to tear the crown from authority's head and then trample it underfoot [Matthew 7:6]. And in addition, he would like to pervert and reduce to nothing all God's works and ordinances. Therefore, we 63
must be watchful and well armed [2 Corinthians 10:4]. We must not allow ourselves to be directed or turned away from the Word, in order that we may not think of Baptism as a mere empty sign, like the fanatic's dream [Jeremiah 23:25].

Lastly, we must also know what Baptism signi- 64
fies and why God has ordained just this outward sign and ceremony for the Sacrament by which
we are first received into the Christian Church.
The act or ceremony is this: we are sunk under 65
the water, which passes over us, and afterward are drawn out again. These two parts, (a) to be sunk under the water and (b) drawn out again, signify Baptism's power and work. It is nothing other than putting to death the old Adam and effecting the new man's resurrection after that [Romans 6:4–6]. Both of these things must take place in us all our lives. So a truly Christian life is nothing other than a daily Baptism, once begun and ever to be continued. For this must be done without ceasing, that we always keep purging away whatever belongs to the old Adam. Then what belongs to the new man may come forth. But what 66

is the old man? It is what is born in human beings from Adam: anger, hate, envy, unchastity, stinginess, laziness, arrogance—yes, unbelief. The old man is infected with all vices and has by nature
67 nothing good in him [Romans 7:18]. Now, when we have come into Christ's kingdom [John 3:5], these things must daily decrease. The longer we live the more we become gentle, patient, meek, and ever turn away from unbelief, greed, hatred, envy, and arrogance.

68 This is Baptism's true use among Christians, as signified by baptizing with water. Therefore, where this is not done, the old man is left unbridled. He continually becomes stronger. That is not using Baptism, but working against Baptism.
69 For those who are without Christ cannot help but become worse daily, just as the proverb says, which expresses the truth "Worse and worse—the
70 longer a vice lasts, the worse it gets." If a year ago someone was proud and greedy, then he is more proud and greedy this year. So the vice grows and increases with him from his youth up. A young child has no special vice. But when it grows up, it becomes unchaste and impure. When it reaches maturity, real vices begin to triumph. The longer the child lives, the more vices.

71 Therefore, the old man goes unrestrained in

his nature if he is not stopped and suppressed by
Baptism's power. On the other hand, where people have become Christians, the old man daily
decreases until he finally perishes. That is truly
being buried in Baptism and daily coming forth
again. Therefore, the outward sign is appointed 72
not only for a powerful effect, but also for an illustration. Therefore, where faith flourishes with 73
its fruit, there it has no empty meaning, but the
work ‹of mortifying the flesh› goes with it [Ro-
mans 8:13]. But where faith is lacking, it remains
a mere unfruitful sign.

Here you see that Baptism, both in its power 74
and meaning, includes also the third Sacrament,
which has been called repentance. It is really
nothing other than Baptism. What else is repen- 75
tance but a serious attack on the old man ‹, that
his lusts be restrained,› and an entering into a
new life? Therefore, if you live in repentance, you
walk in Baptism. For Baptism not only illustrates
such a new life, but also produces, begins, and
exercises it. For in Baptism are given grace, the 76
Spirit, and power to suppress the old man, so that
the new man may come forth and become strong
[Romans 6:3–6].

Our Baptism abides forever. Even though 77
someone should fall from Baptism and sin, still

we always have access to it. So we may subdue
78 the old man again. But we do not need to be sprinkled with water again [Ezekiel 36:25–26; Hebrews 10:22]. Even if we were put under the water a hundred times, it would still be only one Baptism, even though the work and sign continue
79 and remain. Repentance, therefore, is nothing other than a return and approach to Baptism. We repeat and do what we began before, but abandoned.

80 I say this lest we fall into the opinion in which we were stuck for a long time. We were imagining that our Baptism is something past, which we can no longer use after we have fallen again into sin. The reason for this is that Baptism is regarded as only based on the outward act once performed
81 ‹and completed›. This arose from the fact that St. Jerome wrote that "repentance is the second plank by which we must swim forth and cross over the water after the ship is broken, on which we step and are carried across when we come
82 into the Christian Church." By this teaching Baptism's use has been abolished so that it can no longer profit us. Therefore, Jerome's statement is not correct, or at any rate is not rightly understood. For the ship of Baptism never breaks, because (as we have said) it is God's ordinance

and not our work [1 Peter 3:20–22]. But it does happen, indeed, that we slip and fall out of the ship. Yet if anyone falls out, let him see to it that he swims up and clings to the ship until he comes into it again and lives in it, as he had done before.

In this way one sees what a great, excellent 83
thing Baptism is. It delivers us from the devil's jaws and makes us God's own. It suppresses and takes away sin and then daily strengthens the new man. It is working and always continues working until we pass from this estate of misery to eternal glory.

For this reason let everyone value his Baptism 84
as a daily dress [Galatians 3:27] in which he is to
walk constantly. Then he may ever be found in
the faith and its fruit, so that he may suppress the
old man and grow up in the new. For if we would 85
be Christians, we must do the work by which we
are Christians. But if anyone falls away from the 86
Christian life, let him again come into it. For just as Christ, the Mercy Seat [Romans 3:25], does not draw back from us or forbid us to come to Him again, even though we sin, so all His treasure and gifts also remain. Therefore, if we have received forgiveness of sin once in Baptism, it will remain every day, as long as we live. Baptism will remain as long as we carry the old man about our neck.

PART 5

THE SACRAMENT OF THE ALTAR

1 Just as we have heard about Holy Baptism, so we must also speak about the other Sacrament, in these same three points: What is it? What are its benefits? and Who is to receive it? And all these points are established through the words by which Christ has instituted this Sacrament.
2 Everyone who desires to be a Christian and go to this Sacrament should know them. For it is not our intention to let people come to the Sacrament and administer it to them if they do not know what they seek or why they come. The words, however, are these:

3 Our Lord Jesus Christ, on the night He was betrayed, took bread, and when He had given thanks, He broke it and gave it to the disciples and said, "Take, eat; this is My body, which is given for you. This do in remembrance of me."

In the same way also, He took the cup after supper, and when He had given thanks, He gave it to them, saying: "Drink of it, all of you; this is My blood of the new testament, which is shed for you for the forgiveness of sins. This do, as often as you drink it, in remembrance of Me."

Here also we do not wish to enter into contro- 4
versy and fight with the defamers and blasphemers of this Sacrament, but to learn first (as we did
with Baptism) what is of the greatest importance.
The chief point is God's Word and ordinance
or command. For the Sacrament has not been
invented nor introduced by any man. Without
anyone's counsel and deliberation it has been
instituted by Christ. The Ten Commandments, 5
the Lord's Prayer, and the Creed keep their nature and worth, even if you never keep, pray, or
believe them. So also this honorable Sacrament
remains undisturbed. Nothing is withdrawn or
taken from it, even though we use and administer it unworthily. Do you think God cares about 6
what we do or believe, as though on that account
He should allow His ordinance to be changed?
Why, in all worldly matters everything stays the
way God has created and ordered it, no matter
how we employ or use it. This point must always 7
be taught, for by it the chatter of nearly all the fa-
natical spirits can be repelled. For they regard the
Sacraments, unlike God's Word, as something
that we do.

8 "Now, what is the Sacrament of the Altar?"

Answer, "It is the true body and blood of our Lord Jesus Christ, in and under the bread and wine, which we Christians are commanded by
9 Christ's Word to eat and to drink." Just as we have said that Baptism is not simple water, so here also we say that though the Sacrament is bread and wine, it is not mere bread and wine, such as are ordinarily served at the table [1 Corinthians 10:16–17]. But this is bread and wine included in, and connected with, God's Word.

10 It is the Word, I say, that makes and sets this Sacrament apart. So it is not mere bread and wine, but is, and is called, Christ's body and blood [1 Corinthians 11:23–27]. For it is said, "When the Word is joined to the element or natural substance, it becomes a Sacrament." This saying of St. Augustine is so properly and so well put that he has scarcely said anything better. The Word must make a Sacrament out of the element, or
11 else it remains a mere element. Now, it is not the word or ordinance of a prince or emperor. But it is the Word of the grand Majesty, at whose feet all creatures should fall and affirm it is as He says, and accept it with all reverence, fear, and humility [Isaiah 45:23; Philippians 2:10].

With this Word you can strengthen your con- 12
science and say, "If a hundred thousand devils,
together with all fanatics, should rush forward,
crying, 'How can bread and wine be Christ's body
and blood?' and such, I know that all spirits and
scholars together are not as wise as is the Divine
Majesty in His little finger" [see 1 Corinthians
1:25]. Now here stands Christ's Word, "Take, eat; 13
this is My body. . . . Drink of it, all of you; this is
My blood of the new testament," and so on. Here
we stop to watch those who will call themselves
His masters and make the matter different from
what He has spoken. It is true, indeed, that if you
take away the Word or regard the Sacrament
without the words, you have nothing but mere
bread and wine. But if the words remain with 14
them, as they shall and must, then, by virtue of
the words, it is truly Christ's body and blood.
What Christ's lips say and speak, so it is. He can
never lie or deceive [Titus 1:2].

It is easy to reply to all kinds of questions about 15
which people are troubled at the present time,
such as this one: "Can even a wicked priest serve
at and administer the Sacrament?" And whatever
other questions like this there may be. For here we 16
conclude and say, "Even though an imposter takes
or distributes the Sacrament, a person still receives

THE SACRAMENT OF THE ALTAR;
FROM 1530 LARGE CATECHISM

the true Sacrament, that is, Christ's true body and
blood, just as truly as a person who ‹receives or›
administers it in the most worthy way." For the
Sacrament is not founded upon people's holiness,
but upon God's Word. Just as no saint on earth,
indeed, no angel in heaven, can make bread and
wine be Christ's body and blood, so also no one
can change or alter it, even though it is misused.
The Word by which it became a Sacrament and 17
was instituted does not become false because of
the person or his unbelief. For Christ does not
say, "If you believe or are worthy, you receive
My body and blood." No, He says, "Take, eat and
drink; this is My body and blood." Likewise, He
says, "Do this" (i.e., what I now do, institute, give,
and ask you, take). That is like saying, "No matter 18
whether you are worthy or unworthy, you have
here His body and blood by virtue of these words
that are added to the bread and wine." Note and 19
remember this well. For upon these words rest all
our foundation, protection, and defense against
all errors and deception that have ever come or
may yet come.

So we have, in a brief way, covered the 20
first point that deals with this Sacrament's essence. Now examine further the effectiveness
and benefits that really caused the Sacrament to

be instituted. This is its most necessary part, so that we may know what we should seek and gain
21 there. This is plain and clear from the words just mentioned, "This is My body and blood, given and shed *for you* for the forgiveness of sins."
22 Briefly, that is like saying, "For this reason we go to the Sacrament: there we receive such a treasure by and in which we gain forgiveness of sins." "Why so?" "Because the words stand here and give us this. Therefore, Christ asks me to eat and drink, so that this treasure may be my own and may benefit me as a sure pledge and token. In fact, it is the very same treasure that is appointed for me against my sins, death, and every disaster."

23 On this account it is indeed called a food of souls, which nourishes and strengthens the new man. For by Baptism we are first born anew [John 3:5]. But, as we said before, there still remains the old vicious nature of flesh and blood in mankind. There are so many hindrances and temptations of the devil and of the world that we often become weary and faint, and sometimes we also stumble [Hebrews 12:3].

24 Therefore, the Sacrament is given as a daily pasture and sustenance, that faith may refresh and strengthen itself [Psalm 23:1–3] so that it will not fall back in such a battle, but become ever stronger

and stronger. The new life must be guided so that 25
it continually increases and progresses. But it 26
must suffer much opposition. For the devil is such
a furious enemy. When he sees that we oppose
him and attack the old man, and that he cannot
topple us over by force, he prowls and moves
about on all sides [1 Peter 5:8]. He tries every trick
and does not stop until he finally wears us out, so
that we either renounce our faith or throw up our
hands and put up our feet, becoming indifferent
or impatient. Now to this purpose the comfort of 27
the Sacrament is given when the heart feels that
the burden is becoming too heavy, so that it may
gain here new power and refreshment.

But here our wise spirits twist themselves 28
about with their great art and wisdom. They cry
out and bawl, "How can bread and wine forgive
sins or strengthen faith?" They hear and know
that we do not say this about bread and wine.
Because, in itself, bread is bread. But we speak
about the bread and wine that is Christ's body
and blood and has the words attached to it.
That, we say, is truly the treasure—and nothing
else—through which such forgiveness is gained.
Now the only way this treasure is passed along 29
and made our very own is in the words "Given
. . . and shed for you." For in the words you have

both truths, that it is Christ's body and blood, and
30 that it is yours as a treasure and gift. Now Christ's body can never be an unfruitful, empty thing that does or profits nothing. Yet, no matter how great the treasure is in itself, it must be included in the Word and administered to us. Otherwise we would never be able to know or seek it.

31 Therefore also, it is useless talk when they say that Christ's body and blood are not given and shed for us in the Lord's Supper, so we could not have forgiveness of sins in the Sacrament. Although the work is done and the forgiveness of sins is secured by the cross [John 19:30], it cannot come to us in any other way than through the Word. How would we know about it otherwise, that such a thing was accomplished or was to be given to us, unless it were presented by preaching or the oral Word [Romans 10:17; 1 Corinthians 1:21]? How do they know about it? Or how can they receive and make the forgiveness their own, unless they lay hold of and believe the Scriptures
32 and the Gospel? But now the entire Gospel and the article of the Creed—I believe in . . . the holy Christian Church, . . . the forgiveness of sins, and so on—are embodied by the Word in this Sacrament and presented to us. Why, then, should we let this treasure be torn from the Sacrament when

the fanatics must confess that these are the very words we hear everywhere in the Gospel? They cannot say that these words in the Sacrament are of no use, just as they dare not say that the entire Gospel or God's Word, apart from the Sacrament, is of no use.

So we have covered the entire Sacrament, both 33
what it is in itself and what it brings and profits. Now we must also see who is the person that receives this power and benefit. That is answered briefly, as we said above about Baptism and often elsewhere: Whoever believes the words has what they declare and bring. For they are not spoken or proclaimed to stone and wood, but to those who hear them, to whom He says, "Take, eat," and so
on. Because He offers and promises forgiveness of 34
sin, it cannot be received except by faith. This faith He Himself demands in the Word when He says, "Given . . . and shed for you, " as if He said, "For this reason I give it, and ask you to eat and drink it, that you may claim it as yours and enjoy it."
Whoever now accepts these words and believes 35
that what they declare is true has forgiveness. But whoever does not believe it has nothing, since he allows it to be offered to him in vain and refuses to enjoy such a saving good. The treasure, indeed, is opened and placed at everyone's door, yes, upon

his table. But it is necessary that you also claim it
36 and confidently view it as the words tell you. This is the entire Christian preparation for receiving this Sacrament worthily. Since this treasure is entirely presented in the words, it cannot be received and made ours in any other way than with the heart. Such a gift and eternal treasure cannot
37 be seized with the fist. Fasting, prayer, and other such things may indeed be outward preparations and discipline for children, so that the body may keep and bring itself modestly and reverently to receive Christ's body and blood. Yet the body cannot seize and make its own what is given in and with the Sacrament. This is done by the faith in the heart, which discerns this treasure and desires it.
38 This may be enough for what is necessary as a general instruction about this Sacrament. What may be said about it further belongs to another time.

39 In conclusion, since we now have the true understanding and doctrine of the Sacrament, there is also need for some admonition and encouragement. Then people may not let such a great treasure—daily administered and distributed among Christians—pass by unnoticed. So those who want to be Christians may prepare to
40 receive this praiseworthy Sacrament often. For we see that people seem weary and lazy about

receiving the Sacrament. A great multitude hears the Gospel. Yet because the nonsense of the pope has been abolished and we are freed from his laws and coercion, they go one, two, three years, or even longer without the Sacrament. They act as though they were such strong Christians that
they have no need of it. Some allow themselves 41
to be hindered and held up by the excuse that we have taught that no one should approach the Sacrament except those who feel hunger and thirst, which drive them to it. Some pretend that it is a matter of liberty and not necessary. They pretend that it is enough to believe without it. For the most part, they go so far astray that they become quite brutish and finally despise both the Sacrament and God's Word.

Now, it is true, as we have said, that no one 42
should by any means be forced or compelled to go to the Sacrament, lest we institute a new murdering of souls. Nevertheless, it must be known that people who deprive themselves of and withdraw from the Sacrament for such a long time are not to be considered Christians. For Christ has not instituted it to be treated as a show. Instead, He has commanded His Christians to eat it, drink it, and remember Him by it.

43 Indeed, those who are true Christians and value the Sacrament precious and holy will drive and move themselves to go to it. We will present something on this point so that the simpleminded and the weak who also would like to be Christians may be more stirred up to consider the cause and need that ought to
44 move them. In other matters applying to faith, love, and patience, it is not enough to teach and instruct alone. There is also need for daily encouragement [Hebrews 10:24–25]. So here also there is need for us to continue to preach so that people may not become weary and disgusted. For we know and feel how the devil always opposes this and every Christian exercise. He drives and deters people from them as much as he can.

45 We have, in the first place, the clear text in Christ's very words, "Do this in remembrance of Me" [Luke 22:19]. These are inviting and commanding words by which all who would be Christians are told to partake of this Sacrament. Therefore, whoever wants to be Christ's disciple, with whom He here speaks, must also consider and keep this Sacrament. They should not act from compulsion, being forced by others, but in obedience to the Lord Jesus Christ, to please Him.
46 However, you may say, "But the words are added, 'As often as you drink it'; there He compels no

one, but leaves it to our free choice." I answer, 47
"That is true, yet it is not written so that we should never do so. Yes, since He speaks the words 'As often as you drink it,' it is still implied that we should do it often. This is added because He wants to have the Sacrament free. He does not limit it to special times, like the Jewish Passover, which they were obliged to eat only once a year. They could only have it on the fourteenth day of the first full moon in the evening [Exodus 12:6, 18]. They still must not change a day." It is as if He would say by these words, "I institute a Passover or Supper for you. You shall enjoy it not only once a year, just upon this evening, but often, when and where you will, according to everyone's opportunity and necessity, bound to no place or appointed time."
But the pope later perverted this and again made 48
the Sacrament into a Jewish feast.

So you see, it is not left free in the sense that we 49
may despise it. I call that despising the Sacrament if one allows a long time to elapse—with nothing to hinder him—yet never feels a desire for it. If you want such freedom, you may just as well have the freedom to not be a Christian and not have to believe or pray. One is just as much commanded by Christ as the other. But if you want to be a Christian, you must from time to time fulfill and

50 obey this commandment. For this commandment ought always to move you to examine yourself [1 Corinthians 11:28; 2 Corinthians 13:5] and to think, "See, what sort of a Christian I am! If I were one, I would certainly have some small longing for what my Lord has commanded me to do."

51 Since we act like strangers toward the Sacrament, it is easy to see what sort of Christians we were under the papacy. We went to the Sacrament from mere compulsion and fear of human commandments, without natural longing and without love, and never thought about Christ's command-
52 ment. But we neither force nor compel anyone. Nor does anyone have to do it to serve or please us. This should lead and constrain you by itself, that the Lord desires it and that it is pleasing to Him. You must not let people force you to faith or any good work. We are doing no more than talking about and encouraging you about what you ought to do—not for our sake, but for your own sake. The Lord invites and allures you. If you despise it, you must answer for that yourself [2 Corinthians 5:10].

53 Now, this is to be the first point, especially for those who are cold and indifferent. Then they may reflect upon it and rouse themselves. For this is certainly true, as I have found in my own experience, and as everyone will find in his own case: if

a person withdraws like this from the Sacrament,
he will daily become more and more callous and
cold, and will at last disregard the Sacrament completely. To avoid this, we must examine our heart 54
and conscience [1 Corinthians 11:28; 2 Corinthians 13:5], and we must act like people who desire
to be right with God [Psalm 78:37]. The more this
is done, the more the heart will be warmed and
enkindled, so it may not become entirely cold.

But if you say, "How can I come if I feel that 55
I am not prepared?" Answer, "That is also my
cause for hesitation, especially because of the old
way under the pope." At that time we tortured
ourselves to be so perfectly pure that God could
not find the least blemish in us. For this reason
we became so timid that we were all instantly
thrown into fear and said to ourselves, "Alas! we
are unworthy!" Then nature and reason begin to 56
add up our unworthiness in comparison with the
great and precious good. Then our good looks
like a dark lantern in contrast with the bright sun,
or like filth in comparison with precious stones.
Because nature and reason see this, they refuse to
approach and wait until they are prepared. They
wait so long that one week trails into another,
and half the year into the other. If you consider 57
how good and pure you are and labor to have no
hesitations, you would never approach.

58 Therefore, we must make a distinction here
between people. Those who are lewd and morally
loose must be told to stay away [1 Corinthians
5:9–13]. They are not prepared to receive forgiveness of sin, since they do not desire it and do not
59 wish to be godly. But the others, who are not such
callous and wicked people, and who desire to be
godly, must not absent themselves. This is true
even though otherwise they are feeble and full of
infirmities. For St. Hilary also has said, "If anyone
has not committed sin for which he can rightly be
put out of the congregation and be considered no
Christian, he ought not stay away from the Sacra-
60 ment, lest he should deprive himself of life." No
one will live so well that he will not have many
daily weaknesses in flesh and blood.

61 Such people must learn that it is the highest art to know that our Sacrament does not depend upon our worthiness. We are not baptized because we are worthy and holy. Nor do we go to Confession because we are pure and without sin. On the contrary, we go because we are poor, miserable people. We go exactly because we are unworthy. This is true unless we are talking about someone who desires no grace and Absolution nor intends to change.

But whoever would gladly receive grace and 62
comfort should drive himself and allow no one to frighten him away. Say, "I, indeed, would like to be worthy. But I come, not upon any worthiness, but upon Your Word, because You have commanded it. I come as one who would gladly be Your disciple, no matter what becomes of my
worthiness." This is difficult. We always have this 63
obstacle and hindrance to encounter: we look more upon ourselves than upon Christ's Word and lips. For human nature desires to act in such a way that it can stand and rest firmly on itself. Otherwise, it refuses to approach. Let this be enough about the first point.

In the second place, there is besides this com- 64
mand also a promise, as we heard above. This ought most strongly to stir us up and encourage us. For here stand the kind and precious words, "This is My body, which is given for you. . . . This is My blood . . . shed for you for the forgiveness of
sins." These words, I have said, are not preached 65
to wood and stone, but to me and you. Otherwise, Christ might just as well be silent and not institute a Sacrament. Therefore consider, and read yourself into this word *you*, so that He may not speak to you in vain.

66 Here He offers to us the entire treasure that
He has brought for us from heaven. With the
greatest kindness He invites us to receive it also
in other places, like when He says in St. Matthew
11:28, "Come to Me, all who labor and are heavy
67 laden, and I will give you rest." It is surely a sin
and a shame that He so cordially and faithfully
summons and encourages us to receive our highest and greatest good, yet we act so distantly toward it. We permit so long a time to pass ‹without
partaking of the Sacrament› that we grow quite
cold and hardened, so that we have no longing
68 or love for it. We must never think of the Sacrament as something harmful from which we had
better flee, but as a pure, wholesome, comforting
remedy that grants salvation and comfort. It will
cure you and give you life both in soul and body.
For where the soul has recovered, the body also is
relieved. Why, then, do we act as if the Sacrament
were a poison, the eating of which would bring
death?

69 To be sure, it is true that those who despise the
Sacrament and live in an unchristian way receive
it to their hurt and damnation [1 Corinthians
11:29–30]. Nothing shall be good or wholesome
for them. It is just like a sick person who on a
whim eats and drinks what is forbidden to him

by the doctor. But those who are mindful of their 70
weakness desire to be rid of it and long for help. They should regard and use the Sacrament just like a precious antidote against the poison that they have in them. Here in the Sacrament you are to receive from the lips of Christ forgiveness of sin. It contains and brings with it God's grace and the Spirit with all His gifts, protection, shelter, and power against death and the devil and all misfortune.

So you have, from God, both the command 71
and the promise of the Lord Jesus Christ. Besides this, from yourself, you have your own distress, which is around your neck. Because of your distress this command, invitation, and promise are given. This ought to move you. For Christ Himself says, "Those who are well have no need of a physician, but those who are sick" [Matthew 9:12]. In other words, He means those who are weary and heavy-laden with their sins, with the fear of death, temptations of the flesh, and of the devil.
If, therefore, you are heavy laden and feel your 72
weakness, then go joyfully to this Sacrament and receive refreshment, comfort, and strength [Mat-
thew 11:28]. If you wait until you are rid of such 73
burdens, so that you might come to the Sacrament
pure and worthy, you must stay away forever. In 74

that case Christ pronounces sentence and says, "If you are pure and godly, you have no need of Me, and I, in turn, no need of you." Therefore, the only people who are called unworthy are those who neither feel their weaknesses nor wish to be considered sinners.

75 But if you say, "What, then, shall I do if I cannot feel such distress or experience hunger and thirst for the Sacrament?" Answer, "For those who are of such a mind that they do not realize their condition I know no better counsel than that they put their hand into their shirt to check whether they have flesh and blood. And if you find that you do, then go, for your good, to St. Paul's Epistle to the Galatians. Hear what sort of a fruit your flesh is:

> Now the works of the flesh are evident: sexual immorality, impurity, sensuality, idolatry, sorcery, enmity, strife, jealousy, fits of anger, rivalries, dissensions, divisions, envy, drunkenness, orgies and things like these. [Galatians 5:19–21]

76 Therefore, if you cannot discern this, at least believe the Scriptures. They will not lie to you, and they know your flesh better than you yourself. Yes, St. Paul further concludes in Romans 7:18, "I know that nothing good dwells in me,

that is, in my flesh." If St. Paul may speak this way
about his flesh, we cannot assume to be better
or more holy than him. But the fact that we do 77
not feel our weakness just makes things worse.
It is a sign that there is a leprous flesh in us that
can't feel anything. And yet, the leprosy rages and
keeps spreading. As we have said, if you are quite 78
dead to all sensibility, still believe the Scriptures,
which pronounce sentence upon you. In short,
the less you feel your sins and infirmities, the
more reason you have to go to the Sacrament to
seek help and a remedy.

In the second place, look around you. See 79
whether you are also in the world, or if you do not
know it, ask your neighbors about it. If you are
in the world, do not think that there will be lack
of sins and misery. Just begin to act as though
you would be godly and cling to the Gospel. See
whether no one will become your enemy, and,
furthermore, do you harm, wrong, and violence,
and likewise give you cause for sin and vice. If
you have not experienced this, then let the Scriptures tell you about it, which everywhere give this
praise and testimony about the world.

Besides this, you will also have the devil about 80
you. You will not entirely tread him under foot
[Luke 10:19], because our Lord Christ Himself

81 could not entirely avoid him. Now, what is the devil? Nothing other than what the Scriptures call him, a liar and a murderer [John 8:44]. He is a liar, to lead the heart astray from God's Word and to blind it, so that you cannot feel your distress or come to Christ. He is a murderer, who
82 cannot bear to see you live one single hour. If you could see how many knives, darts, and arrows are every moment aimed at you [Ephesians 6:16], you would be glad to come to the Sacrament as often as possible. But there is no reason why we walk about so securely and carelessly, except that we neither think nor believe that we are in the flesh and in this wicked world or in the devil's kingdom.

83 Therefore, try this and practice it well. Be sure to examine yourself [1 Corinthians 11:28], or look about you a little, and just keep to the Scriptures. If even then you still feel nothing, you have even more misery to regret both to God and to your brother. Then take this advice and have others pray for you. Do not stop until the stone is removed from your heart [Ezekiel 36:25–26].
84 Then, indeed, the distress will not fail to become clear, and you will find that you have sunk twice as deep as any other poor sinner. You are much more in need of the Sacrament against the misery

which, unfortunately, you do not see. With God's grace, you may feel your misery more and become hungrier for the Sacrament, especially since the devil doubles his force against you. He lies in wait for you without resting so that he can seize and destroy you, soul and body. You are not safe from him for one hour. How soon he can have you brought suddenly into misery and distress when you least expect it!

Let this, then, be said for encouragement, 85
not only for those of us who are old and grown, but also for the young people, who ought to be brought up in Christian doctrine and understanding. Then the Ten Commandments, the Creed, and the Lord's Prayer might be taught to our youth more easily. Then they would receive them with pleasure and seriousness, and so they would use them from their youth and get used
to them. For the old are now nearly past this op- 86
portunity. So these goals and others cannot be reached unless we train the people who are to come after us and succeed us in our office and work. We should do this in order that they also may bring up their children successfully, so that God's Word and the Christian Church may be
preserved. Therefore, let every father of a fam- 87
ily know that it is his duty, by God's order and

command, to teach these things to his children, or to have the children learn what they ought to know [Ephesians 6:4]. Since the children are baptized and received into the Christian Church, they should also enjoy this communion of the Sacrament, in order that they may serve us and be useful to us. They must all certainly help us to believe, love, pray, and fight against the devil.